An Introduction to

CLASSICAL AND CONTEMPORARY SOCIAL THEORY:

A Critical Perspective

THE REYNOLDS SERIES IN SOCIOLOGY

Larry T. Reynolds, *Editor*

by **General Hall, Inc.**

An Introduction to
CLASSICAL AND CONTEMPORARY SOCIAL THEORY:
A Critical Perspective

Berch Berberoglu
University of Nevada, Reno

Second Edition

General Hall, Inc.
Publishers
5 Talon Way
Dix Hills, New York 11746

An Introduction to Classical and Contemporary Social Theory:
A Critical Perspective

GENERAL HALL, INC.
5 Talon Way
Dix Hills, New York 11746

Publisher: Ravi Mehra
Composition: Perfect Setting, Bridgehampton, NY

LIBRARY OF CONGRESS CATALOG CARD NUMBER: **98-71778**

ISBN: 1-882289-55-2 [paper]
1-882289-56-0 [cloth]

ISBN 1-882289-56-0

Manufactured in the United States of America

Contents

PREFACE AND ACKNOWLEDGMENTS

Social theory is an essential tool that scholars use in their analysis of society. Just as without thinking we cannot make sense of the world around us, without the use of theory facts in their raw form remain unintelligible and disjointed to all but the purest of the pure empiricists, who reject the use of theory altogether. The adoption of a theoretical approach in social analysis, especially one that is critical and challenges long-held assumptions about the social world, is therefore an important first step in developing an informed understanding of society through social research.

My interest in social theory goes back more than two decades, when I was first introduced to the great social theorists of the nineteenth and early twentieth centuries in my undergraduate theory course taught by Larry Reynolds at Central Michigan University in the early 1970s. It is through his inspiring and engaging lectures on Emile Durkheim, Max Weber, Karl Marx, and other giants of classical social theory that I came to confront some of the central social issues of our time. Later, in a graduate seminar on contemporary social theory, I learned from Larry about the raging controversies in American sociology—from its early beginnings to the Chicago School to Talcott Parsons, Robert Merton, and other proponents of modern functionalism, which dominated the postwar academic scene, to C. Wright Mills and the critical and radical theorizing and activism of a new generation of sociologists in the 1960s who made an important and lasting contribution to the discipline.

The knowledge I gained through my formal theoretical training in these formative years, however, goes much beyond what I learned about individual theorists, for my broad exposure to social theory during this critical period helped establish a solid foundation for my theoretical studies in the years that followed. For his pivotal role in introducing me to some of the central theoretical positions that I have come to adopt over the years, and in this way for setting me on a most valuable intellectual journey, I thank my mentor, colleague, and friend Larry Reynolds in appreciation of his contribution to my theoretical development.

During my graduate studies in the early to mid-1970s, first at the State University of New York at Binghamton and then at Central Michigan University, where I attended seminars and courses taught by James Petras and Blain Stevenson, respectively, and later at the University of Oregon, where I studied toward my doctoral degree under Albert Szymanski, my exposure to and interest in social theory, centered in political economy and class analysis, came to define the parameters of my theoretical orientation in sociology. In this more mature period in my thinking I came to adopt a more developed, dialectical conception of social analysis informed by the principles of historical materialism. It was also during this most critical period in my intellectual development that I began to see the central, indeed most fundamental, role played by social class in society. Analysis of class structure, class conflict, and class struggle, defined in terms of relations of production, became the basis of my approach to social theory and social research that continues to inform my theoretical perspective and intellectual work. Throughout this book, the analysis of the positions of each of the classical and contemporary theorists discussed is carried out from the vantage point of this most fundamental social phenomenon—*class*.

This book was written with the aim of introducing to the beginning college student some of the major classical and contemporary social theorists of the late nineteenth and early twentieth centuries. Given both the number of prominent social theorists and the scope of the issues addressed over the past century, this book is necessarily selective in both focus and depth of analysis of questions raised by a select number of theorists I have decided to cover. Moreover, the analysis presented is both interpretative and critical in its approach toward the subject matter. It is hoped that such an approach will stimulate interest in the beginning student to ponder the critical issues raised by these theorists in a fresh new way. In this sense, the book is not intended as a definitive text in social theory but as a supplemental guide for use in introductory sociology and social theory courses to help familiarize students with the works of some of the most prominent social theorists of our time.

The twenty chapters that make up this book were designed to be brief, concise, and to the point, expressed whenever possible in the words of the theorists concerned so that the central ideas of each of these theorists can be presented in their original form. Thus this introductory book on social theory was designed to serve as an initial stepping-stone to more in-depth analyses of these and other theorists usually covered in more advanced texts specifically prepared for advanced undergraduate theory courses in sociology. If this book succeeds in stimulating in the beginning student a modicum of interest in social theory—one that will lead to further theoretical studies—then the purpose for which this project was originally conceived and undertaken will be worth all the effort I have put into it.

Over the years, many colleagues have contributed to the formation and development of the ideas presented in these pages and thus have contributed, directly or indirectly, to the success of this undertaking. I would like to thank Jim Salt, Walda Katz-Fishman, Judy Aulette, Jerry Lembcke, Martha Gimenez, John Leggett, Bill Domhoff, Julia Fox, Alan Spector, Jan Fritz, David Dickens,

Karl Kreplin, David L. Harvey, and Johnson Makoba for their contributions to discussions on various currents in classical and contemporary social theory.

I would like to thank Laurie Smith for typing several chapters of this book, Irene Glynn for doing an excellent job in copyediting the manuscript, and Ravi Mehra, my publisher, for his exemplary professional work in every stage of the publication process.

This second edition is a revised and expanded edition of the original volume first published in 1993. Although there are clear limitations to the scope of any project of this sort, five new chapters have been added to this edition. These include chapters on: Cooley and Mead on Human Nature and Society; Homans on Social Exchange; Goffman and Garfinkel on Dramaturgy, Ethnomethodology, and Everyday Life; Wilson and Willie on Race, Class, and Poverty; and Harvey and Callinicos on Postmodernism and Its Critique. The first three of these chapters were written by Larry Reynolds, Alice Littlefield, and Nancy Herman, respectively, with Larry Reynolds as co-author of the second and third chapters. The remaining chapters were written by me.

I would like to thank my colleagues at the Sociology Department, University of Nevada, Reno for their continued intellectual support over the past two decades, which permitted me to pursue my scholarly work in a most rewarding way.

I would especially like to thank Ann Ronald, Dean of the College of Arts and Science, University of Nevada, Reno for nominating me to become Foundation Professor of Sociology, and the University of Nevada, Reno Foundation Board of Trustees for conferring upon me the honor of being named 1995–1998 Foundation Professor to join the ranks of those few selected for this most prestigious award for excellence in research and creative activity at this university. This revised and expanded edition constitutes one part of my scholarly work during the course of my Foundation Professorship, which has been generously funded by the University of Nevada, Reno Foundation.

This book is dedicated to my introductory sociology and social theory students, who have, over the years, urged me to undertake this project—a task that I gladly undertook to meet this need.

INTRODUCTION

The origins of modern social theory goes back to the classical Greek philosophers Aristotle, Socrates, and Plato, who had an important influence on subsequent generations of social theorists through the Enlightenment to the late nineteenth and early twentieth centuries. While great social thinkers like Jean Jacques Rousseau, who became one of the leading theorists of the Enlightenment, developed their ideas on the foundations of rationalist and empiricist modes of thought dominant in the seventeenth century, they also generated their own uniquely eighteenth-century concept of society and social relations by integrating into their social analysis the scientific discoveries of thinkers like Isaac Newton, who revolutionized the study of nature and set forth a new standard for scientific research.[1]

The intellectual climate of this period was further enhanced by the French Revolution, which brought an added optimism to the improvement of the human condition. These developments in the eighteenth century, however, led to the conservative reaction of the early nineteenth century and at the same time marked a shift in direction of social theory, ushering in the social thought of a new stream of theorists—David Hume, Immanuel Kant, Edmund Burke, and Georg Wilhelm Friedrich Hegel.[2]

The postrevolutionary period gave rise, above all, to the emergence not only of a conservative reaction—which, as in the theories of Louis de Bonald and Joseph de Maistre, advocated a return to the prerevolutionary medieval social order—but to two other strands of thought, one that adhered to the preservation of the existing order, as in the case of Auguste Comte, and another that went beyond the status quo in the direction of an egalitarian social order embracing what Karl Marx later called a form of "utopian socialism," as in the case of Henri Comte de Saint-Simon.[3] These two strands established, by the mid-nineteenth century, the conservative and liberal/radical paths that came to define the parameters of competing traditions in the formation of modern sociological theory.

The collective contributions to social theory of the great thinkers of past centuries evolved by the late nineteenth and early twentieth centuries into the alternative theoretical perspectives of Durkheim, Weber, and Marx, which most sociologists view as having marked a major turning point in classical social theory. These three intellectual giants developed their thinking in direct response to the great social transformations of the eighteenth and nineteenth centuries, a period when the full implications and consequences of life in capitalist society were becoming apparent in all their social, economic, and political dimensions.[4] It was Karl Marx who first developed a comprehensive analysis of the fundamental contradictions of capitalism and established the parameters of discussion and debate on the nature of society and the social order that others, among them Emil Durkheim, Max Weber, Gaetano Mosca, George Herbert Mead, and Sigmund Freud, later came to address.[5] In fact, as Irving Zeitlin has pointed out in his *Ideology and the Development of Sociological Theory*, Marx's work provoked a response that accounts for much of the theoretical arguments developed by these and other social theorists of this period and prompted, as Zeitlin puts it, "the intense debate with his [Marx's] ghost," one that has shaped, "in a large measure, the character of Western sociology."[6]

Analysis of the various explanations given by classical social theorists concerning the nature of society and social relations provides us with an occasion to examine briefly three fundamentally different theoretical approaches, or what Thomas Kuhn has called paradigms,[7] in classical and contemporary social theory: (1) the organic approach; (2) the individualistic approach; and (3) the organizational approach.

The organic approach, adopted by Durkheim, emphasizes the study of social order. Society in this context is conceived as an organism functioning much as the human body, where the various parts making up the organism contribute to the maintenance of the organism as a whole. Thus, for the smooth functioning of society, each part making up the system must function in organic harmony with the whole. Social order, consensus, equilibrium, and maintenance of the status quo are the central questions taken up for study; and disorganization of the family structure, breakdown of the moral order (especially of religion), as well as the decline in traditional cultural values are social problems typically studied by this approach. Culture, tradition, and long-held social values, seen as the primary motive force of social life, define the source and logic of social relations within this conservative conception of society and the social order, where society is viewed as an entity greater than the individuals who comprise it.

The individualistic approach, which Weber adopted as a theoretical expression of the newly emergent capitalist social order, gives primacy to the individual as the motive force of social development. Based on the logic of competition, private enterprise, and individualism as the defining characteristics of the new society in the making, this approach concentrates on the individual as the unit of analysis, emphasizing the importance of such concepts as the actor, personality, the self, motivation, and adaptation. Although Weber and a few others in this tradition also addressed larger, structural phenomena, such as status, authority, and bureaucracy, the heavy reliance of this approach on human nature as the motive force of society and social relations gives this approach primarily a micro-level orientation, where problems affecting society are defined in terms of individual deviance, maladjustment, and other problems that can be solved only by the successful reintegration of the individual into the existing social order.

Finally, the organizational approach, articulated by Marx, emphasizes the centrality of social organization and focuses on class relations and class struggles as the motive force of social change and social transformation. This approach highlights the exploitation of labor as the most important, indeed the central, problematic of capitalist society—one that is based on class conflict and class struggles. The nature of society and the social order, as well as the position of individuals within it, are viewed in terms of the dominant mode of production determined by the social relations of production (or class relations), which define the parameters of the course and direction of broader social relations in society. Instead of the integration of the individual into the dominant culture and morality, as in the conservative organic position, or the adaptation of the individual into society through control of personal deviation from social norms, as in the liberal individualistic position, Marx's organizational approach contends that it is not the individual but society based on class inequalities, hence class conflict, that is the source of social tensions and instability. Thus, class struggles and struggles for political power are the collective expression of individuals adversely affected in society, individuals who eventually organize and struggle collectively to improve their situation and thereby advance their interests.

The political implications of the three approaches can be delineated rather clearly if one places them in their proper historical context. While all three schools of thought developed in direct response to the changing social, economic, and political conditions in the eighteenth and nineteenth centuries, these schools represented the interests of diverse classes that came to define the social context of a declining or ascending order in a most crucial period of epochal social transformation—the transition from feudalism to capitalism and the consolidation of capitalist rule in the nineteenth century.

The organic approach was a conservative reaction to the newly emergent capitalist order and advocated a return to the old feudal system, wherein society functioned around established traditional cultural precepts, where the church was supreme, and where the individual was bound to the moral values of the medieval order. Viewing the rising capitalist system as a formula for moral decadence and social decline, the proponents of the organic approach thus argued in favor of social cohesion and social solidarity, which they felt were characteristic of the old moral code.

The individualistic approach, in contrast, lent its support to the rising capitalist order wherein old traditions were giving way to individual self-advancement in a market-oriented economy founded on private ownership of the means of production, competition, and individualism. The individualistic school viewed the decline of the old order as a step forward in human freedom—freedom from bondage to the church or any other moral authority that dictated the terms of social life, and freedom to accumulate private capital in accordance with the laws of the market. Thus this approach was conducive to and in effect came to advance the interests of the capitalist class as against the feudal landlords on the one hand and the wage-earning working class on the other.

Finally, the organizational approach, while supportive of the limited human freedoms achieved under the new social order, criticized the amassing of wealth from private profit based on the exploitation of labor. Thus it threw its lot with the oppressed and exploited laboring masses it believed would eventually become conscious of their class interests and struggle for the abolition of private property and private profit through a revolutionary transformation of capitalist society, establishing in its place an egalitarian social order.

Durkheim, Weber, and Marx thus provided three alternative responses to the burning questions of their time and thereby established the parameters of these competing perspectives at the broader theoretical level. These approaches have come to play a central role in the development of social theory over the past century, incorporating the contributions of many of the social theorists included in this book, and are viewed by most sociologists today as representing the best elements of classical and contemporary social theory.[8]

This book is divided into two parts. Part I focuses on classical social theory and examines the works of fifteen social theorists of the late nineteenth and early twentieth centuries. Part II provides an analysis of the works of twenty contemporary social theorists of the middle to late twentieth century. The book concludes with some reflections on the nature of social theory and its central role in critical intellectual discourse.

The theories examined in the chapters that make up this book present a sampling of the rich traditions of both classical and contemporary social theory. By providing an overview of the works of some of the most important theorists of the nineteenth and twentieth centuries, the book addresses a variety of controversial theoretical issues that have brought social theorizing to the forefront of critical analysis.

Notes

1. Jean Jaques Rousseau, *The Social Contract* (New York: Dutton, 1950).
2. See, for example, David Hume, *A Treatise of Human Nature* (Oxford: Claredon Press, 1949); Immanuel Kant, *Critique of Pure Reason* (New York: St. Martin's Press, 1929); Edmund

Burke, *Reflections on the Revolution in France* (New Rochelle, N.Y.: Arlington House, n.d.); G.W.F. Hegel, *The Philosophy of History* (New York: Dover, 1956); and idem, *Science of Logic* (London: Allen and Unwin, 1969).

3. Auguste Comte, *The Positive Philosophy*, 2 vols. (London: Kegan Paul, 1893); Henri de Saint-Simon, *Social Organization, the Science of Man and Other Writings* (New York: Harper and Row, 1964).

4. For an excellent discussion of the changes taking place in Western Europe during this period, see Maurice Dobb, *Studies in the Development of Capitalism* (New York: International Publishers, 1963). See also Karl Polanyi, *The Great Transformation* (Boston: Beacon, 1957).

5. See Karl Marx, *Capital*, 3 vols. (New York: International Publishers, 1967).

6. Irving M. Zeitlin, *Ideology and the Development of Sociological Theory* (Englewood Cliffs, N.J.: Prentice Hall, 1968), viii.

7. Thomas S. Kuhn, *The Structure of Scientific Revolutions*, 2nd ed. (Chicago: University of Chicago Press, 1970).

8. See, for example, David L. Westby, *The Growth of Sociological Theory* (Englewood Cliffs, N.J.: Prentice Hall, 1991).

PART I
CLASSICAL SOCIAL THEORY

Chapter 1

MARX AND ENGELS ON SOCIAL CLASS AND CLASS STRUGGLE

Karl Marx (1818–83) and Frederick Engels (1820–95), the most prominent and controversial social theorists of the nineteenth century, provided an analysis of social classes and class struggles in society aimed at understanding the root causes of class inequality based on the exploitation of labor. The analysis of class structure, exploitation, and class struggle, they stressed, must be placed within the framework of the dynamics of social change in the world historical process. The crucial task for them, therefore, was to identify and examine the primary motive force of social transformation that defined the parameters of societal development: *class struggle*. Hence, to understand the centrality of class and class struggle in the Marxist analysis of society and social structure, we first briefly discuss the methodological foundation of the Marxist approach—dialectical and historical materialism.

Dialectical and Historical Materialism

The dialectical method, developed by G.W.F. Hegel, explains phenomena in terms of an endless process of transformation of contradictions resulting from the unity of opposites (i.e., thesis vs. antithesis leading to synthesis). Whereas Hegel applied the dialectical approach to the realm of *ideas* (i.e., the clash of ideas *A* and *B* giving rise to idea *C*), Marx and Engels adapted it to the realm of the material world to explain the interaction between ideas (theory) and social reality (practice). Going a step further, Marx and Engels transformed Hegel's dialectical idealism into their materialist dialectics by placing ideas in their social, material context. By applying it to the real world, they were able to explain the structure of social relations which, in class society, is based on the struggle between opposing *classes*.

Advancing their materialist conception of social reality, Marx and Engels argued that the material condition of human beings—their real-life experience, their social existence—determines their consciousness. Consequently, the social reality in which humans live molds their thought:

> The production of ideas, of conceptions, of consciousness is at first directly interwoven with the material activity and the material intercourse of men, the language of real life. Conceiving, thinking, the mental intercourse of men, appear at this stage as the direct efflux of their material behavior. The same applies to mental production as expressed in the language of the politics, laws, morality, religion, metaphysics of a people.[1]

Elsewhere, Marx states clearly that "it is not the consciousness of men that determines their being, but on the contrary, their social being that determines their consciousness."[2] Thus the material world is prior to and a necessary condition for the emergence of consciousness.

Criticizing Hegel's idealist conception of dialectics, Marx and Engels point out that

> in direct contrast to German philosophy which descends from heaven to earth, here we ascend from earth to heaven. That is to say, we do not set out from what men say, imagine, conceive, nor from men as narrated, thought of, imagined, conceived, in order to arrive at men in the flesh. We set out from real, active men, and on the basis of their real life-process we demonstrate the development of the ideological reflexes and echoes of this life-process.[3]

The starting point in Marx and Engels's analysis of society and social relations is the recognition of human beings as the prime agents of material production—a process that forms the basis of production and reproduction of human existence. As they put it:

> Life involves before everything else eating and drinking, a habitation, clothing and many other things. The first historical act is thus the production of the means to satisfy these needs, the production of material life itself.[4]

Hence, in the early stages of history, principal human needs were based on and centered in subsistence for the sustenance of life.

Through time, humans created and developed tools, skills, knowledge, and work habits—in short, *the forces of production*—to an extent that permitted, for the first time, the accumulation of surplus. Although in most of human history, for thousands of years, human beings lived in classless primitive-communal societies, the accumulation of a social surplus in the form of a surplus product gave rise to the emergence of classes in society. With the development of social classes and class inequality, there emerged historically specific social *relations of production*, or class relations, between those who produced the surplus and those who claimed ownership and control of that surplus (e.g., slaves vs. masters; serfs vs. landlords; wage laborers vs. capitalists). Marx and Engels pointed out that the forces of production (including the labor process at the point of production) and the social relations of production (class relations) together constitute a society's *mode of production*, or its social-economic foundation, defined as the way in which a society's wealth is produced and distributed-in short, the social-economic system (e.g., slavery, feudalism, capitalism).

Applying these concepts to history and examining the material conditions surrounding the production and reproduction process, in effect the very basis of life itself, Marx and Engels observed that:

> The way in which men produce their means of subsistence depends first of all on the nature of the actual means they find in existence and have to reproduce. This mode of production must not be considered simply as being the reproduction of the physical existence of the individuals. Rather it is a definite form of activity of these individuals, a definite form of expressing their life, a definite *mode of life* on their part. As individuals express their life, so they are. What they are, therefore, coincides with their production, both with what they produce and with how they produce. The nature of individuals thus depends on the material conditions determining their production.[5]

Engels, in a letter to Heinz Starkenburg, further explains the historical materialist outlook on society this way:

> What we understand by the economic conditions which we regard as the determining basis of the history of society are the methods by which human beings in a given society produce their means of subsistence and exchange the products among themselves (in so far as division of labour exists). Thus the *entire technique* of production and transport is here included. According to our conception this technique also determines the method of exchange and, further, the division of products and with it, after the dissolution of tribal society, the division into classes also and hence the relations of lordship and servitude and with them the state, politics, law, etc.[6]

Once a class society emerges—in which the production process is firmly established, a surplus is generated, and social classes have developed—the relations of production (or class relations) become the decisive element defining the nature of the dominant mode of production, which in turn gives rise to the political *superstructure*, including first and foremost the state, as well as other political and ideological institutions that serve the interests of the propertied classes in society. Thus the superstructure arises from and becomes a reflection of the dominant mode of production, which reinforces the existing social order, notwithstanding the fact that the superstructure itself may influence or otherwise effect changes in favor of the long-term interests of the dominant classes in society.[7] As Marx points out:

> In the social production of their life, men enter into definite relations that are indispensable and independent of their will, relations of production which correspond to a definite stage of development of their material productive forces. The sum total of these relations of production constitutes the economic structure of society, the real foundation, on which rises a legal and political superstructure and to which correspond definite forms of social consciousness.[8]

For Marx, then, the *relations of production*, that is, the "relationship of the owners of the conditions of production to the direct producers," as he defines it, "reveals the innermost secret, the hidden basis of the entire social structure, and with it . . . the corresponding specific form of the state."[9] The relations of production, as the decisive element in the mode of production, together with the political superstructure that emerges from it, thus constitute the very basis of the analysis of social classes, class structure, class struggles, and social transformation, according to the Marxist classics.

Social Class and Class Struggle

The focal point stressed by Marx and Engels in explaining social class and class struggle is that an analysis of property-based unequal social relations prevalent in the organization of material production in class society is the key to an understanding of the nature of a particular social order. The position of people in the production process, situated according to their relation to the ownership/control of the means of production, is viewed by Marx and Engels as the decisive element defining class relations in society. It is from these historically-specific social relations of production that inequalities precisely arise and lead to class conflict and class struggles, that is, struggles for political power. Thus, referring to class society, "the history of all hitherto existing society," Marx and Engels point out, "is the history of class struggles."[10]

In capitalist society, for example, two main classes relate to one another in the production sphere: capitalists (owners of capital) and workers (wage labor). The capitalist class owns the means of production and accumulates capital through the exploitation of labor. The working class does not own the means of production but instead uses its labor power to generate value for the capitalists as a condition for its survival. As Marx and Engels point out, capitalist society is thus mainly divided into:

> the class of modern capitalists, owners of the means of social production and employers of wage-labor . . . [and] the class of modern wage-laborers who, having no means of production of their own, are reduced to selling their labor-power in order to live.[11]

Under capitalist production, while a portion of the value generated by labor is returned to it for subsistence (wages), a much greater portion goes to the capitalist in the form of surplus value (profits), which, accumulated over time, enhances the wealth and fortunes of the capitalist class visà-vis all other classes in society, especially the working class, in both relative and absolute terms.[12]

The accumulation of capital through this process of exploitation under capitalism thus results in disparities in wealth and income between labor and capital and eventually leads to conflict and struggle between the two classes, extending to realms beyond the production sphere itself. Hence, in this class struggle, write Marx and Engels,

> oppressor and oppressed stood in constant opposition to one another, carried on an uninterrupted, now hidden, now open fight, a fight that each time ended, either in a revolutionary reconstitution of society at large, or in the common ruin of the contending classes.[13]

Marx and Engels conceptualized class at three different yet related levels: economic, social, and political. The first of these is identified as the foundation of class analysis, class-in-itself *(Klasse-an-sich)*. This refers to groups of people who relate to production in the same way, that is, those who have the same property relationships in the productive process (e.g., workers, peasants, landlords, capitalists). Structurally, then, *class-in-itself* is the logical outcome of the mode of production in all class societies.

At the next, sociological, level is what can be referred to as *social class*. A class-in-itself becomes a social class only when there is a close relationship between the members of a particular class. In this sense, industrial workers (the classic proletariat) constitute a social class in that not only do the members of this class interact in the productive process (in factories, under socialized conditions of production) but they also have a distinct culture, lifestyle, habits—in short, a cohesive intraclass association, including intermarriage between members of the same class.

Finally, the third and highest level of class is referred to by Marx as that of class-for-itself *(Klasse-für-sich)*. This means that a *Klasse-an-sich* that has become a social class has attained full consciousness of its interests and goals and engages in common political activity in pursuit of its class interests.

Thus in capitalist society, the dominant capitalist class, through its control of the major superstructural institutions, obtains political control and disseminates ruling-class ideology, hence assuring its ideological hegemony in society.

At the same time, to prevent the development of class consciousness among the masses and to neutralize and divert their frustration and anger against the system, the dominant class facilitates the development of false consciousness among the working class. This, in turn, serves to block the development of class consciousness among workers and thus prevents, to the extent it is successful, the potential for social revolution.

Nevertheless, the material conditions of life under capitalism eventually incite workers to organize and rise up. As the working class becomes class conscious and discovers that its social condition is the result of its exploitation by the capitalists, it invariably begins to organize and fight back to secure for itself economic benefits and political rights denied in capitalist society—a society wherein the exploitation of labor through the extraction of surplus value is legally assured by the capitalist state.

This exploitation, hence domination, of the working class by capital, Marx points out, would, sooner or later, lead to class struggle, that is, a struggle for political power: "The conflict between proletariat and bourgeoisie is a struggle of one class against another, a struggle that means in its highest expression a total revolution."[14] "Is there any reason to be surprised," Marx asks, "that a society based on class conflict leads to brutal opposition, and in the last resort to a clash between individuals?"[15] "An oppressed class," he maintains, "is the condition of existence of every society based on class conflict. Thus the liberation of the oppressed class necessarily involves the creation of a new society," adding "only in an order of things in which there are no class conflicts will social evolutions cease to be political revolutions."[16]

Political Power and the State

Political power, Marx and Engels point out, grows out of economic (class) power driven by money and wealth, but to maintain and secure their wealth, dominant classes of society establish and control political institutions to hold down the masses and assure their continued domination. The supreme superstructural institution that historically has emerged to carry out this task is the state.

The emergence of the state coincided with the emergence of social classes and class struggles resulting from the transition from a primitive communal to more advanced modes of production when an economic surplus was first generated. Ensuing struggles over control of this surplus led to the development of the state; once captured by the dominant classes in society, the state became an instrument of force to maintain the rule of wealth and privilege against the laboring masses, to maintain exploitation and domination by the few over the many. Without the development of such a powerful instrument of force, there could be no assurance of protection of the privileges of a ruling class, who clearly lived off the labor of the masses. The newly wealthy needed a mechanism that

> would not only safeguard the newly-acquired property of private individuals against the communistic traditions of the gentile order, would not only sanctify private property, formerly held in such light esteem, and pronounce this sanctification the highest purpose of human society, but would also stamp the gradually developing new forms of acquiring property, and consequently, of constantly accelerating increase in wealth, with the seal of general public recognition; an institution that would perpetuate, not only the newly-rising class division of society, but also the right of the possessing class to exploit the non-possessing classes and the rule of the former over the latter.
>
> And this institution arrived. The *state* was invented.[17]

Thus the state developed as an institution as a result of the growth of wealth and social classes:

> Former society, moving in class antagonisms, had need of the state, that is, an organization of the exploiting class at each period for the maintenance of its external conditions of production; that is, therefore, for the forcible holding down of the exploited class in the conditions of oppression (slavery, villeinage or serfdom, wage labor) determined by the existing mode of production. The state was the official representative of society as a whole, its embodiment in a visible corporation; but it was this only in so far as it was the state of that class which itself, in its epoch, represented society as a whole; in ancient times, the state of the slave-owning citizens; in the Middle Ages, of the feudal nobility; in our epoch, of the bourgeoisie.[18]

In *The Origins of the Family, Private Property and the State*, Engels writes:

> It is, as a rule, the state of the most powerful, economically dominant class, which, through the medium of the state, becomes also the politically dominant class, and thus acquires new means of holding down and exploiting the oppressed class. Thus, the state of antiquity was above all the state of the slave owners for the purpose of holding down the slaves, as the feudal state was the organ of the nobility for holding down the peasant serfs and bondsmen, and the modern representative state is an instrument of exploitation of wage labor by capital.[19]

Thus, in all class-divided societies throughout history, "political power is merely the organized power of one class for oppressing another."[20]

In modern capitalist society, the state, reflecting the interests of the dominant capitalist class, can thus be identified as the *capitalist state*, for as Marx and Engels point out, this state is nothing more than a political organ of the bourgeoisie adopted for the "guarantee of their property and interests."[21] Hence, "the bourgeoisie has . . . conquered for itself, in the modern representative State, exclusive political sway. The executive of the modern State is but a committee for managing the common affairs of the whole bourgeoisie."[22] In this sense, the struggle of the working class against capital takes on both an economic and a political content:

> The more it [the state] becomes the organ of a particular class, the more it directly enforces the supremacy of that class. The fight of the oppressed class against the ruling class becomes necessarily a political fight, a fight first of all against the political dominance of this class.[23]

Seen in this context, the centrality of the state as an instrument of *class rule* takes on an added importance in the analysis of social class and class struggles, for political power contested by the warring classes takes on its real meaning in securing the rule of the victorious class when that power is ultimately exercised through the instrumentality of the state.

Conclusion

We have seen that for Marx and Engels the concepts of social class and class struggle are central to their analysis of society and social relations. Moreover, their interest in class structure is a result of their larger quest to understand the dynamics of social change and social transformation within the world historical process. In this context, their understanding of the motive force of historical progress and the agents of societal change have brought to the fore the question of political power and the state. Thus, Marx and Engels's focus on production relations, informing their concept of social class, exploitation, and class struggle, as the foundation of the historical materialist conception of society and social life, including the role of the state and power relations in society, makes an important contribution to classical social theory as well as to our understanding of class structure in modern society. In fact, as we see in subsequent chapters, many of the prominent social theorists of the late nineteenth and much of the twentieth century were either influenced by the theories of Marx and Engels or developed their own theories in direct opposition to those of the Marxist classics.

Notes

1. Karl Marx and Frederick Engels, *The German Ideology* (New York: International Publishers, 1947), 13–14.

2. Karl Marx, "Preface to *A Contribution to the Critique of Political Economy,*" in K. Marx and F. Engels, *Selected Works* (New York: International Publishers, 1972), 182.

3. Marx and Engels, *German Ideology*, 14.

4. Ibid., 16.

5. Ibid., 7.

6. Frederick Engels, "Letter to Heinz Starkenburg" in K. Marx and F. Engels, *Selected Correspondence* (New York: International Publishers, 1935), 516.

7. See Marx and Engels, *German Ideology*; Karl Marx, *The Poverty of Philosophy* (New York: International Publishers, 1963); Marx, "Preface to *A Contribution to a Critique of Political Economy*,"; Karl Marx, Capital, vol. 3 (Moscow: Foreign Languages Publishing House, 1962); Frederick Engels, *Anti-Duhring* (New York: International Publishers, 1976), pt. 2; and other writings of Marx and Engels.

8. Marx, "Preface to *A Contribution to a Critique of Political Economy*," 182.

9. Marx, *Capital*, 3:772.

10. Karl Marx and Frederick Engels, "Manifesto of the Communist Party," in Marx and Engels, *Selected Works*, 35.

11. Ibid.

12. Surplus value (or gross profits) is that part of the total value created by labor that workers surrender to the owners of the means of production after receiving only a small portion of the total value in the form of wages. Although the end result is the same, the extraction of surplus value from the producers takes on different forms in social formations dominated by different, historically-specific mode(s) of production.

13. Marx and Engels, "Manifesto," 36.

14. Marx quoted in Ralph Dahrendorf, *Class and Class Conflict in Industrial Society* (Stanford: Stanford University Press, 1959), 18.

15. Ibid.

16. Ibid.

17. Frederick Engels, *The Origin of the Family, Private Property and the State* (New York: International Publishers, 1972), 263.

18. Engels, *Anti-Duhring*, 306.
19. Engels, *The Origin*.
20. Marx and Engels, "Manifesto," 53.
21. Marx and Engels, *German Ideology*, 59.
22. Marx and Engels, "Manifesto," 37.
23. Frederick Engels, "Ludwig Feuerbach and the End of Classical German Philosophy," in Marx and Engels, *Selected Works*, 627.

Chapter 2

DURKHEIM ON SOCIETY AND THE SOCIAL ORDER

Emile Durkheim (1858–1917), one of the eminent social theorists of the late nineteenth and early twentieth centuries, has with a select few other theorists shared center stage in classical sociological theory during the past century. Together with the two other giants of classical social theory—Karl Marx and Max Weber—Durkheim has left his mark in sociology as one of the great social thinkers of our time.

This chapter examines the major ideas set forth by Durkheim concerning human nature, society, and the social order. Limited in scope, our analysis focuses on Durkheim's attempt to develop an organic theory of society.[1]

Human Nature

Durkheim, in advancing his sociological critique of Western industrial society and its impact on the quality of individual and social life, made a number of key assumptions about human nature that were fundamentally different from and opposed to those of Marx and Engels. Thus, to understand Durkheim and his theory of society and social structure, we must first understand his underlying assumptions about human nature.

"Our first duty," writes Durkheim in his major work *The Division of Labor in Society*, "is to make a moral code for ourselves."[2] This moral code is crucial, he argues, because it constitutes the very foundation of social solidarity:

> [Moral] discipline . . . is a code of rules that lays down for the individual what he should do so as not to damage collective interests and so as not to disorganize the society of which he forms a part. . . . It is this discipline that curbs him, that marks the boundaries, that tells him what his relations with his associates should be, where illicit encroachments begin, and what he must pay in current dues towards the maintenance of the community.[3]

But why does Durkheim suggest that we need such a system of social control? Further, why is it "necessary" that the creative expression of individuals be curbed? "The interests of the individual," writes Durkheim, "are not those of the group he belongs to and indeed there is often a real antagonism between the one and the other."[4] Moreover,

> these social interests that the individual has to take into account are only dimly perceived by him: sometimes he fails to perceive them at all, because . . . he is not constantly aware of them, as he is of all that concerns and interests himself. It seems, then, that there should be some system which brings them to mind, which obliges him to respect them, and this system can be no other than a moral discipline.[5]

Durkheim's argument here is both basic and simple: To promote and advance the larger (social) interests of the group and to limit excessive self-interest, the individual must be guided by a "moral code" that implants such values throughout society. To be effective, the adoption of a "moral discipline," he stresses, must take place during early childhood socialization. Durkheim makes this point quite clear when he says:

> Education must help the child understand at an early point that, beyond certain contrived boundaries that constitute the historical framework of justice, there are limits based on the nature of things, that is to say, in the nature of each of us. This has nothing to do with insidiously inculcating a spirit of resignation in the child; or curbing his legitimate ambitions; or preventing him from seeing the conditions existing around him. Such proposals would contradict the very principles of our social system. But he must be made to understand that the way to be happy is to set proximate and realizable goals, corresponding to the nature of each person and not to attempt to reach objectives by straining neurotically and unhappily toward infinitely distant and consequently inaccessible goals.[6]

Thus through moral discipline "and by means of it alone," Durkheim assures us, "are we able to teach the child to rein in his desires, to set limits to his appetites of all kinds, to limit and, through limitation, to define the goals of his activity."[7] Hence moral discipline, defined in this way, becomes a mechanism of social control that fulfills the need for integration, conformity, and, in the final analysis, harmony between the individual and society, which in turn helps preserve order in society as a whole.

Durkheim argues that the individual's egoism, if left unchecked, becomes a dangerous force against societal integration and stability. Without a moral commitment to society, the individual, writes Durkheim, fails to strengthen his or her ties to the community. The long-term consequences of such "anomie," or alienation, he argues, is "excessive individualism," the prime cause of "egoistic suicide."

> Excessive individualism not only results in favoring the action of suicidogenic causes, but it is itself such a cause. It not only frees man's inclination to do away with himself from a protective obstacle, but creates this inclination out of whole cloth and thus gives birth to a special suicide which bears its mark.[8]

Such an eventuality "results from the fact that society is not sufficiently integrated at all points to keep all its members under its control."[9] Thus discipline is necessary, Durkheim insists, not only for the maintenance of social order but for the individual's happiness and moral health as well.

Durkheim's concept of the individual and his or her role in society is, therefore, essentially based on the notion of *conformity*. Only through conformity, according to Durkheim, will both society and the individual be able to survive. Thus, if the lack of conformity leads to serious social and psychological problems, "the only remedy for the ill," such as egoistic suicide, "is to restore enough consistency to social groups for them to obtain a firmer grip on the individual, and for him to feel himself bound to them."[10] Hence it is the duty of the individual, Durkheim stresses, to be a "good" citizen, a "good" and "productive" worker, and contribute to the social collectivity. To what type of social collectivity, or society, however, Durkheim never tells us.[11]

In attempting to integrate his moralistic theory of society with real conditions of social existence, Durkheim argues that his "good" and contributing citizen must tolerate oppression; this he does through implication:

> The less one has the less he is tempted to extend the range of his needs indefinitely. Lack of power, compelling moderation, accustoms men to it. . . . [Poverty] is actually the best school for teaching self-restraint. Forcing us to constant self-discipline, it prepares us to accept collective discipline with equanimity.[12]

But why is such an authoritative position granted to society? Why is such an emphasis placed on discipline, self-restraint, and adaptation of the individual to an established moral code or standard in society? And what if such a code is against the interests of the majority of the people in that society?[13]

Society and the Social Order

Durkheim's concept of society is essentially a deterministic one; he views society as an all-embracing, independent entity, independent of the individuals that constitute the social collectivity. Society in Durkheim's theoretical scheme becomes a real force, having a life of its own. Thus the structural separation of the "collective conscience" from interaction among individuals at the everyday level means that individuals lack control of their own destiny, and their daily life experiences constitute the manifestation of forces shaping the definition of the greater social reality: "The individual is dominated by a moral reality greater than himself: namely, collective reality."[14]

Likening the nature and functions of society to that of the human organism, Durkheim introduced the notion of "the organic analogy," an idea contending that

> there are a large number of parallels between the functioning of a human organism, with its brain, central nervous system, cells, muscles, and heart and that of a society, with its ideas, classes, division of labor, and culture. The relations among the parts of society are thought to be similar to those among the organs of a human body. As the human body is an organism in which the whole is greater than the sum of its parts, societies can be viewed as social organisms in which their wholes are greater than the sums of their parts. If societies, like human bodies, are viewed as functioning organically, then each subpart must have a function—that is, a role—in contributing to the survival of the entire organism.[15]

Stressing the superiority of society over the individual, Durkheim argues that the individual should conform to the dictates of society in order to preserve the social organism:

> Since the superiority of society to him is not simply physical but intellectual and moral, it has nothing to fear from a critical examination. By making man understand by how much the social being is richer, more complex, and more permanent than the individual being, reflection can only reveal to him the intelligible reasons for the subordination demanded of him and for the sentiments of attachment and respect which habit has fixed in his heart.[16]

Referring to social institutions as the collective expression of forces that make up society, Durkheim points out that these institutions

> will no longer be regarded simply as characterless, ineffective ideological arrangements. Rather they will be felt to be real, living, active forces which, because of the way they determine the individual, prove their independence of him; which, if the individual enters as an element in the combination whence these forces ensue, at least control him once they are formed.[17]

Thus, for Durkheim, society is superior to and determines the behavior of the individuals that make up the social whole. Accordingly, the individual, Durkheim asserts, must subordinate himself to the larger community if society is to function properly.

Going a step further, Durkheim argues that it is society "that draws us out of ourselves, that obliges us to reckon with other interests than our own":

> It is society that has taught us to control our passions, our instincts, to prescribe law for them, to restrain ourselves, to deprive ourselves, to sacrifice ourselves, to subordinate our personal ends to higher ends.[18]

Society, defined in this way, is for Durkheim a sacred, religious entity. Thus, "Religion," writes Durkheim,

> ceases to be an inexplicable hallucination and takes a foothold in reality. In fact, we can say that the believer is not deceived when he believes in the existence of a moral power upon which he depends and from which he receives all that is best in himself; this power exists, it is society.[19]

The primary function of religion, according to Durkheim, is to contribute toward the integration of society to encourage a deep sense of moral conformity:

> [Religion] . . . is a system of ideas within which the individuals represent to themselves the society of which they are members, and the obscure but intimate relations which they have with it. This is its primary function; and though metaphorical and symbolic, this representation is not unfaithful. Quite on the contrary, it translates everything essential in the relations which are to be explained: for it is an eternal truth that outside of us there exists something greater than us, with which we enter into communion.
>
> That is why we can rest assured in advance that the practices of the cult, whatever they may be, are something more than movements without importance and gestures without efficacy. By

> the mere fact that their apparent function is to strengthen the bonds attaching the believer to his god, they at the same time really strengthen the bonds attaching the individual to the society of which he is a member, since the god is only a figurative expression of the society.[20]

Thus, in Durkheim's language, the functions of "religion," "god," and "society" become one and the same: They all represent forces of integration, cohesion, conformity, and, in the final analysis, *order* in society. Here, once again, we see another of Durkheim's repeated attempts to reify society: Society, he writes,

> has the chief interest in order and peace; if anomie is an evil, it is above all because society suffers from it, being unable to live without cohesion and regularity. A moral or juridical regulation essentially expresses, then, social needs that society alone can feel.[21]

Thus Durkheim tells us that to maintain harmony between individuals and between them and their society, what is needed is a strong sense of social solidarity.

In *The Division of Labor in Society* Durkheim discusses two kinds of solidarity: (1) mechanical and (2) organic. Mechanical solidarity is based on "states of conscience which are common to all the members of the same society."[22] Thus it is rooted in likenesses and collective sentiments. "Solidarity which comes from likenesses," writes Durkheim, "is at its maximum when the collective conscience completely envelops our whole conscience and coincides in all its points with it."[23] To clarify the nature of this type of solidarity further, Durkheim points out that "at the moment this solidarity exercises its force, our personality vanishes, as our definition permits us to say, for we are no longer ourselves, but the collective life."[24]

What Durkheim is pointing to in this passage is the conflict between the collective conscience and the individual. How can this conflict be resolved within the framework of mechanical solidarity? It can be resolved, according to Durkheim, only by moving to a higher level of solidarity, that which he calls "organic." And the division of labor is the mechanism that raises society to that higher level. Thus the division of labor plays a positive role and becomes the principal social bond among the members of advanced societies, one that reconciles the interests of both the individual and society. Durkheim writes:

> Since mechanical solidarity progressively becomes enfeebled, life properly social must decrease or another solidarity must slowly come in to take the place of that which has gone. The choice

> must be made. In vain shall we contend that the collective conscience extends and grows stronger at the same time as that of individuals. . . . Social progress, however, does not consist in a continual dissolution. On the contrary, the more we advance, the more profoundly do societies reveal the sentiment of self and of unity. There must, then, be some other social link which produces this result; this cannot be any other than that which comes from the division of labor. . . . It is the division of labor which, more and more, fills the role that was formerly filled by the common conscience. It is the principal bond of social aggregates of higher types.[25]

In Durkheim's view, then, the division of labor—the specialization of societal functions—brings about two important developments: (1) it enhances one's individuality through detachment from the "common conscience," while (2) it assures a higher level of social solidarity as a result of the assignment of specific functions to individual members of society.

Conclusion

This chapter has attempted to present a brief statement of Durkheim's views concerning human nature and society. And in the process of our analysis we have examined his major theoretical positions regarding society and the social order, developed as a response to the harsh realities of social life under capitalism in the late nineteenth and early twentieth centuries—a response that represents a clear statement of an ideological position transformed into a conservative social theory that Durkheim attempted to develop in order to contribute to the remedy of problems engendered by emergent industrial capitalism. Although his critique of early capitalist society is laden with attempts to develop a new morality to maintain order in society—hence in this sense it has conservative political implications—his analysis of the dynamics of society and the social order during this period has broader significance with regard to its overall contribution to classical social theory.

Notes

1. See, for example, Robert N. Bellah, "Durkheim and History," *American Sociological Review* 24, no. 4 (August 1959): 447–60; Anthony Giddens, *Capitalism and Modern Social Theory* (New York: Cambridge University Press, 1971); Kurt H. Wolff, ed., *Emile Durkheim, 1858–1917*, (Columbus, Ohio: Ohio State University Press, 1960).
2. Emile Durkheim, *The Division of Labor in Society* (New York: Free Press, 1964), 409.

3. Emile Durkheim, *Professional Ethics and Civic Morals* (Glencoe, Ill.: Free Press, 1958), 14–15.

4. Ibid., 14.

5. Ibid.

6. Emile Durkheim, *Moral Education* (New York: Free Press of Glencoe, 1961), 49.

7. Ibid., 43.

8. Emile Durkheim, *Suicide: A Study in Sociology* (New York: Free Press, 1951), 210.

9. Ibid., 373.

10. Ibid.

11. We assume here that Durkheim means *any* society, including the exploitative capitalist society in which he himself lived.

12. Durkheim, *Suicide*, 254.

13. As, for example, with regard to slaves in slaveowning societies and workers in capitalist society, to cite only two cases that raise serious questions about an approach that plays a legitimizing role vis-à-vis the maintenance of order in society.

14. Durkheim, *Suicide*, 38.

15. James W. Russell, *Introduction to Macrosociology* (Englewood Cliffs, N.J.: Prentice Hall, 1992), 90–91.

16. Emile Durkheim, *The Rules of the Sociological Method* (New York: Free Press, 1964), 123.

17. Durkheim, *Suicide*, 38–39.

18. Emile Durkheim, *Education and Sociology* (Glencoe, Ill.: Free Press, 1956), 76.

19. Emile Durkheim, *The Elementary Forms of Religious Life* (London: Allen & Unwin, 1957), 225.

20. Ibid., 225–26.

21. Durkheim, *The Division of Labor in Society*, 5.

22. Ibid., 109.

23. Ibid., 130.

24. Ibid.

25. Ibid., 173.

Chapter 3

WEBER ON BUREAUCRACY, POWER, AND SOCIAL STATUS

Max Weber (1864–1920) is considered by many to be one of the greatest social theorists of the late nineteenth and early twentieth centuries. While he was influenced by the great social thinkers of his period, Weber developed a distinct approach to the analysis of the state, bureaucracy, and power—an approach that constitutes an alternative to both Durkheimian and Marxist conceptions of power, politics, and society.[1]

This chapter focuses on Weber's theory of bureaucracy, power, class, and status and provides us with an analysis of their relationship in developing an understanding of the Weberian approach to the study of society.

Bureaucracy

What distinguishes Weber's analysis of bureaucracy from that of Marx and lends itself to an affinity with classical elite theory is his attempt to assign a *quasi*-autonomous role to the state wherein the bureaucrats appear to be serving their own interests, and the bureaucracy appears to be a power unto itself, with more and more permanent features. Operating at this secondary, institutional level, "bureaucracy," writes Weber, "is a power instrument of the first order," and adds that "where the bureaucratization of administration has been completely carried through, a form of power relation is established that is practically unshatterable."[2]

In Weber's view, bureaucracies are large-scale, impersonal organizations in which power relations are organized in a top-down hierarchical manner for purposes of efficiently attaining centrally defined goals. Thus bureaucratic discipline "is nothing but the consistently rationalized, methodically prepared and exact execution of the received order, in which all personal criticism is unconditionally suspended and the actor is unswervingly and exclusively set for carrying out the command."[3]

"The decisive reason for the advance of bureaucratic organization," Weber writes, "has always been its purely *technical* superiority over any other form of organization."[4]

> The fully developed bureaucratic apparatus compares with other organizations exactly as does the machine with the non-mechanical modes of production. Precision, speed, unambiguity, knowledge of the files, continuity, discretion, unity, strict subordination, reduction of friction and of material and personal costs—these are raised to the optimum point in the strictly bureaucratic administration, and especially in its monocratic form.[5]

Outlining Weber's description of the general characteristics of a bureaucratic administrative staff, David L. Westby provides a summary list of the structural features of bureaucratic organization and the characteristics of bureaucratic officialdom as follows:

A. *Organizational features:*

1. Official jurisdictional areas ordered by rules, so that organizational activities are assigned as official duties delimited in a stable way by rules and continuously fulfilled.
2. An established hierarchy of authority under a central authority.
3. Separation of office from private domicile and performance of organizational duties on the basis of written documents maintained in files.
4. Office management presupposes specialized training as the basis for employment.
5. Organizational activities become full-time.
6. Management proceeds according to general rules, the knowledge of which "represents a special technical expertise."

B. *Characteristics of officialdom:*

1. The holding of office is a vocation, meaning that incumbency is based on training and evidence of competence, and that the official is oriented to discharge of office as a "duty."
2. There is a strong relationship between certain organizational characteristics and the extent to which office incumbency determines the status position of the official.
3. The official is appointed.
4. Tenure tends to be for life. This has the effect of contributing to the performance of the organization, but may affect the social status of the official and the technical efficiency of the organization negatively.
5. The official is remunerated by a money salary (and so a money economy is a presupposition of a bureaucracy).
6. The official moves through a career within the organizational hierarchy. This, along with (4) and (5) contributes to the creation of office sinecures in the form of prebends.[6]

In this context of the nature of bureaucratic administration, Weber notes the rise to prominence of the "expert" as a logical outcome of the growth of society and of bureaucracy: "The more complicated and specialized modern culture becomes, the more its external supporting apparatus demands the personally detached and strictly objective expert."[7] Through the possession of technical knowledge, the expert is able to obtain "a position of extraordinary power." Moreover, "bureaucratic organizations, or the holders of power who make use of them," Weber continues, "have the tendency to increase their power still further by the knowledge growing out of experience in the service."[8] But "expertise alone does not explain the power of bureaucracy"; equally important is the bureaucrats' possession of "official information" to which they and they alone have direct access-something that Weber sees as the "supreme power instrument" of the bureaucracy.[9]

The bureaucratic form of social organization, Weber argues, thus lends itself to control and domination of society and the individuals within it and generates as a by-product a social alienation that puts managers and workers, bureaucrats and citizens, in opposite camps, thus leading to conflict between those who control and govern and those who are controlled and governed at all levels of society.

Given their logic and organizational structure, bureaucracies, Weber believed, often take on lives of their own, which are often beyond the control of individual bureaucrats who take part in their daily operation. Thus, according to Weber, once a bureaucracy is firmly in place, it becomes a political force that can very seldom be successfully dismantled or eliminated.

> The individual bureaucrat cannot squirm out of the apparatus into which he has been harnessed. . . . In the great majority of cases he is only a small cog in a ceaselessly moving mechanism which prescribes to him an essentially fixed route of march. . . .
>
> The ruled, for their part, cannot dispense with or replace the bureaucratic apparatus once it exists. . . . Increasingly the material fate of the masses depends upon the continuous and correct functioning of the ever more bureaucratic organizations of private capitalism, and the idea of eliminating them becomes more and more utopian.[10]

The key question then becomes one of determining *who* controls and directs the complex bureaucratic machine. Unlike Robert Michels, Weber does *not* believe bureaucracy is, in essence, an autonomous power unto itself; rather, it is a tool or instrument of power:

> The bureaucratic structure goes hand in hand with the concentration of the material means of management in the hands of the

> master. This concentration occurs, for instance, in a well-known and typical fashion in the development of big capitalist enterprises, which find their essential characteristics in this process. A corresponding process occurs in public organizations.[11]

Thus, "the consequences of bureaucracy," Weber concludes, "depend therefore upon the direction which *the powers using the apparatus* give to it."[12] Weber's statement here could be interpreted in two possible ways: one that assigns primacy to the *political* process and grants a special role to the bureaucrats—as individuals and as a group—who manage the day-to-day affairs of the political apparatus, and another where the source of power is located outside the narrow confines of the political institutions in which individual bureaucrats and the bureaucracy as a whole operate—that is, the economy and class structure of society.

It is not surprising that most contemporary Weberians have separated Weber's analysis of bureaucracy from his generalized theory of class and power in society and thus have managed to give a conservative twist to his otherwise controversial analysis. Viewed within a broader societal context, however, it becomes clear that bureaucracy and political power to Weber are the manifestations of the real social forces that dominate the social-economic structure of modern society. Thus, to give primacy to the analytic strength of these secondary political concepts would mean one is dealing with surface phenomena. This is clearly evident, for example, in the works of most contemporary theorists of complex organizations, where power is consistently located within the structure of specific bureaucratic organizations, while bureaucracies are given a logic of their own and are conceived in terms of their special power and dynamics. But, to Weber, to understand more fully the logic of bureaucracy and political control one must examine the nature of property, income, status, and other dimensions of class relations, in society. It is here, in his differential conceptualization of class, status, and power based on market relations that one finds a uniquely Weberian approach in classical social theory.

Class, Status, and Power

It is often pointed out by the proponents of the Weberian approach that Weber's theory of stratification and inequality is "multidimensional." By this is meant that Weber utilized a number of equally important concepts to explain social structure and social inequality. The key variables in his conceptual scheme are class, status, and power.

To Weber, "a 'class' is any group of persons occupying the same class status" or situation.[13] "We may speak of a 'class,'" he writes, "when (1) a number of people have in common a specific causal component of their life chances, in so far as (2) this component is represented exclusively by economic interests in the possession of goods and opportunities for income, and (3) is represented under the conditions of the commodity or labor markets."[14] Central to Weber's conceptualization of class is the notion of "life chances," by which he means "the kind of control or lack of it which the individual has over goods or services and existing possibilities of their exploitation for the attainment of receipts within a given economic order."[15]

In the Weberian formulation of class, "class situation" is ultimately "market situation": "According to our terminology," writes Weber, "the factor that creates 'class' is unambiguously economic interest, and indeed, only those interests involved in the existence of the 'market.'"[16]

One's "class situation," then, is expressed by one's access to "a supply of goods, external living conditions, and personal life experiences"—all of which are derivative of and determined by the amount of control one has and which is exercised in the acquisition of income within a particular economic order. And at the center of this control lies, according to Weber, the key (economic) variable "property."

"'Property' and 'lack of property,'" argues Weber, are "the basic categories of all class situations."[17] In this formulation, one's life chances are "primarily determined by the differentiation of property holdings" and power is derived from the ownership and control of property "which gives [the owners] a monopoly to acquire [highly valued] goods."[18] And since the specific life chances of individuals is created by "the way in which the disposition over material property is distributed, . . . this mode of distribution monopolizes the opportunities for profitable deals for all those who [possess property]."[19]

Although Weber's conception of "property" is somewhat different than the Marxist definition, and that consequently such conception necessarily alters the analytical boundaries of the Weberian definition of the nature, position, and politics of specific classes, it does nonetheless point to the centrality of property relations in the control and execution of power in society.[20]

In addition to the "property class," which constitutes the determinant core of Weber's class analysis, Weber distinguishes two other classes that make up the totality of his class concepts: "acquisition class" and "social class."[21]

> A class is an "acquisition class" when the class situation of its members is primarily determined by their opportunity for the exploitation of services on the market; the "social class" structure is composed of the plurality of class statuses between which an interchange of individuals on a personal basis or in the course of generations is readily possible and typically observable.[22]

While "acquisition classes" are based on occupational criteria, as opposed to property ownership, "social classes" are largely a product of the combination of occupational and property classes: the "working" class, the "lower middle" classes, the "intelligentsia," and "the classes occupying a privileged position through property and education."[23]

We cannot here go into a detailed description of each one of these classes, but suffice it to say that Weber, both in the case of property and acquisition classes, further subdivides them into "positively privileged" and "negatively privileged" classes and adds an intermediate category, making up the "middle class." As Weber puts it:

> Positively privileged property classes typically live from property income. This may be derived from property rights in human beings as with slaveowners, inland, in mining property, in fixed equipment such as plant and apparatus, in ships, and as creditors in loan relationships. . . . Finally, they may live on income from securities.
>
> Class interests which are negatively privileged with respect to property . . . are themselves objects of ownership, that is they are unfree [such as slaves].[24]

Although monopoly control over goods, services, wealth, education, high official position, income, accumulated surplus, and other privileges in the hands of the "positively privileged" property class and lack of such control and appropriation on the part of the "negatively privileged" property class place Weber's analytic scheme in a position that is in a sense analogous to the Marxist conception of exploiting and exploited classes, the logic of such classification is based on an entirely different set of conceptual definitions that separate the two traditions.[25]

"Social status" and "power" are two other major variables in the Weberian theoretical scheme, and we examine them briefly. "Social status," according to Weber, rests on "a typically effective claim to positive or negative privilege with respect to social prestige" derived from "one or more of the following bases: *(a)* mode of living, *(b)* a formal process of education . . . and the acquisition of the corresponding, modes of life, or *(c)* on the prestige of birth, or of an occupation."[26] Thus, within this framework, a social *"stratum,"* then, "is a plurality of individuals who, within a larger group, enjoy a particular kind and level of prestige by virtue of their position."[27] As Weber puts it elsewhere:

> One might thus say that "classes" are stratified according to their relations to the production and acquisition of goods; whereas "status groups" are stratified according to the principles of their *consumption* of goods as represented by special "styles of life."[28]

And, as it is clear from Weber's repeated emphasis throughout his writings, *social status* is a manifestation of class situation, rooted in property relations, and thus is a derivative of class status.

Finally, the third major concept that is central to the Weberian theoretical scheme is "power." "In general, we understand by 'power,'" writes Weber, "the chance of a man or of a number of men to realize their own will in a communal action even against the resistance of others who are participating in the action."[29] Hence, although economic power is the single most important determinant of power as such, it may itself "be the consequence of power existing on other grounds." What is more, "power, including economic power, may be valued 'for its own sake.'" And, "very frequently the striving for power is also conditioned by the social 'honor' it entails."[30] "Indeed," adds Weber, "social honor, or prestige, may even be the basis of political or economic power, and very frequently has been."[31] But, nonetheless, viewed in its ultimate totality, it is economic power based on property ownership that is the crucial determinant of all power in society, according to Weber.

Conclusion

So, what do we make of Weber's position on bureaucracy, stratification, and class inequality? And what is the relationship between his key concepts, bureaucracy, class, status, and power, vis-à-vis the social collectivity? As we have previously noted and as the implications of the foregoing analysis make sufficiently clear, although Weber viewed these concepts as being relatively independent of one another, he did, nonetheless, stress that, in the final analysis, bureaucratic control, social status, and political power are dependent on and determined by *class*, that is, economic power.

On another level, Weber attempted to deal with a specific manifestation of economic power, namely, power accumulated and exercised at the administrative level of large organizations. He observed that the (vertical) means of administration of large organizations were becoming the dominant fact in all branches of modern society, and the type of organization becoming predominant was the bureaucracy. To be able to sort out clearly the source and linkages of power as it pertains to bureaucratic control, however, it is within the context of Weber's analysis of class structure that his position on bureaucracy must be understood. Framed in this way, we can more clearly comprehend the relationship between bureaucracy, class, power, and property in Weber's theory of modern society—one which has made a great contribution to classical social theory.

Notes

1. The relationship between the economy, the state, religion and other spheres of social life are discussed by Weber in his early (1905) work *The Protestant Ethic and the Spirit of Capitalism*

(New York: Scribners, 1948). Here Weber examines the relationship between Protestantism and the rise of capitalism and concludes that Protestantism played a key role in facilitating the development of capitalism in directly challenging the feudal system prevalent under medieval Catholicism in Europe during this period.

2. Max Weber, *From Max Weber, Essays in Sociology*, trans., ed., and with an intro. by H.H. Gerth and C. Wright Mills (New York: Oxford University Press, 1967), 228.

3. Max Weber, *Economy and Society*, 3 vols., ed. Guenther Roth and Claus Wittich (New York: Bedminster Press, 1968), 3:1149.

4. Ibid., 973.

5. Ibid.

6. David L. Westby, *The Growth of Sociological Theory* (Englewood Cliffs, N.J.: Prentice Hall, 1991), 430. For an extended discussion of the characteristics of bureaucratic administration and staff, see Weber, *Economy and Society*, 3:956–63.

7. Ibid., 975.

8. Ibid., 1:225.

9. Ibid., 3:1418.

10. Ibid., 987–88.

11. Ibid., 980.

12. Weber, *From Max Weber*, 230; emphasis added.

13. Max Weber, *The Theory of Social and Economic Organization*, ed. and with an intro. by Talcott Parsons (New York: Free Press, 1964), 424.

14. Weber, *From Max Weber*, 181.

15. Weber, *The Theory of Social and Economic Organization*, 424.

16. Weber, *From Max Weber*, 183.

17. Ibid., 182.

18. Ibid.

19. Ibid., 181–82.

20. See Weber, *The Protestant Ethic and the Spirit of Capitalism*. As we have pointed out earlier, in the Weberian approach classes, including "property classes," are defined in terms of one's "market situation," whereas in Marxist theory class relations are based on social relations of production. See chapter 1 above.

21. Weber, *The Theory of Social and Economic Organization*, 424.

22. Ibid.

23. Ibid., 427.

24. Ibid., 425.

25. For further discussion on this point, see chapter 1.

26. Weber, *The Theory of Social and Economic Organization*, 428.

27. Ibid., 428–29.

28. Weber, *From Max Weber*, 193; emphasis in the original.

29. Ibid., 180.

30. Ibid.

31. Ibid.

Chapter 4

PARETO, MOSCA, AND MICHELS ON ELITES AND MASSES

This chapter focuses on the political theories of three influential classical social theorists of the early twentieth century: Vilfredo Pareto, Gaetano Mosca, and Robert Michels. Together their work on elite formation and oligarchic rule constitutes the core of the classical bureaucratic elite theory of politics.

Classical elite theory maintains that all societies are ruled by elites and that the state is the political instrument by which the vast majority is ruled. This is so, according to this view, because the masses are inherently incapable of governing themselves; therefore, society must be led by a small number of individuals (the elite) who rule on behalf of the masses.

Elites and Their Circulation

In his major work, *The Mind and Society*, Vilfredo Pareto (1848–1923) set out to identify a minority of highly talented individuals at the top levels of society who possessed superior personal qualities and wielded great social and political power; distinguishing this group from the great masses of the people, Pareto called it the *"élite"*.[1] "So let us make a class of the people who have the highest indices in their branch of activity," wrote Pareto, "and to that class give the name of *élite*."[2] Further elaborating on the internal composition of this group, he divided the elite into two (political and social) segments:

> A *governing élite*, comprising individuals who directly or indirectly play some considerable part in government, and a *non-governing élite*, comprising the rest. . . .
>
> So we get two strata in a population: (1) a lower stratum, the *non-élite*, with whose possible influence on government we are not just here concerned; then (2) a higher stratum, *the élite*, which is divided into two: *(a)* a governing *élite*, *(b)* a non-governing *élite*.[3]

Within this framework, the fundamental idea set forth and developed by Pareto was that of the "circulation of elites." By this, Pareto meant two diverse processes operative in the perpetual continuity of elite rule: (1) the process in which *individuals* circulate between the elite and the nonelite; and (2) the process in which a *whole elite* is replaced by a new one.

The main point of Pareto's concept of the circulation of elites is that the ongoing process of replenishment of the governing elite by superior individuals from the lower classes is a critical element securing the continuation of elite rule.

> The governing class is restored not only in numbers, but—and that is the more important thing—in quality, by families rising from the lower classes and bringing with them the vigor and the proportions of residues necessary for keeping themselves in power.[4]

A breakdown in this process of circulation of elites, however, leads to such serious instability in the social equilibrium that "the governing class crashes to ruin and often sweeps the whole of a nation along with it."[5]

In Pareto's reasoning, a "potent cause of disturbance in the equilibrium is the accumulation of superior elements in the lower classes and, conversely, of inferior elements in the higher classes."[6] Hence, "every *élite* that is not ready to fight to defend its position is in full decadence; there remains nothing for it to do but to vacate its place for another *élite* having the verile qualities which it lacks."[7]

Thus, Pareto reaches an inescapable conclusion in his four-volume study: "Aristocracies do not last. Whatever the causes, it is an incontestable fact that after a certain length of time they pass away. History is a graveyard of aristocracies."[8]

The consequences of developments in society are such that they eventually lead to total social transformation, according to Pareto. "Revolutions," he writes,

> come about through accumulations in the higher strata of society . . . of decadent elements no longer possessing the residues suitable for keeping them in power, and shrinking from the use of force; while meantime in the lower strata of society elements of superior quality are coming to the fore, possessing residues suitable for exercising the functions of government and willing enough to use force.[9]

Pareto's explanation of the nature and dynamics of elite rule and their circulation, therefore, rests in large part on the personal qualities of individuals in both elite and nonelite segments of society and their willingness or failure to use force to acquire and retain political power.

Pareto's concern with the decline in legitimacy of the existing order in Italy in the early decades of this century, together with the rising popularity of Marxism which he opposed, drove him to fascism. "Fascism, for Pareto," writes Irving Zeitlin,

> seemed not only to confirm his theories but also to hold out hope for a "new era." That he identified with the new order is borne out by the fact that on March 23, 1923, he accepted an appointment as senator—a position he had declined to accept in the pre-fascist government. In a letter to an acquaintance at the time of acceptance, he wrote: "I am happy to see that you are favorably disposed to the new regime, which, in my opinion, is the only one capable of saving Italy from innumerable evils." And, in the same vein, "France will save herself only if she finds her own Mussolini."[10]

"In general," Zeitlin continues, "Pareto's attitude seems to have been that since the pre-fascist regime did not, or could not, save the country from 'anarchy' by legal means, fascism had to do it by force."[11]

The Political Elite

The fundamental idea that Gaetano Mosca (1858–1941) wanted to develop in his major work, *The Ruling Class*, was a new *political* theory of power. Like Pareto, he divided people in all societies into essentially two distinct classes: the ruling class (the political elite) and the class that is ruled (the masses). The ruling class always enjoys a monopoly of political power over the masses and directs society according to its own interests:

> In all societies . . . two classes of people appear—a class that rules and a class that is ruled. The first class, always the less numerous, performs all political functions, monopolizes power and enjoys the advantages that power brings, whereas the second, the more numerous class is directed and controlled by the first, in a manner that is now more or less legal, now more or less arbitrary and violent.[12]

This is not merely so with every known society of the past and the present; *all* societies *must* be so divided. Herein lies Mosca's argument for the "universal necessity" and "inevitability" of elite rule:

> Absolute equality has never existed in human societies: Political power never has been, and never will be, founded upon the explicit

> consent of majorities. It always has been, and it always will be, exercised by organized minorities, which have had, and will have, the means, varying as the times vary, to impose their supremacy on the multitudes.[13]

Mosca attempts here to establish "the real superiority of the concept of the ruling, or political, class," to show that "the varying structure of ruling classes has a preponderant importance in determining the political type, and also the level of civilization, of the different peoples."[14] Hence for Mosca it is the political apparatus of a given society and an organized minority (i.e., the political elite) that controls this apparatus—not the class structure—that determines the nature and movement of society and societal change.[15]

At one point, Mosca writes that "the discontent of the masses might succeed in deposing a ruling class," but, he immediately adds, "inevitably . . . there would have to be another organized minority within the masses themselves to discharge the functions of a ruling class."[16] As Mosca viewed the specific "functions" of ruling classes in universal terms, he could not envision a state and a society at the service of the laboring masses, as against a ruling class or an "organized minority within the masses."

Mosca's tautological arguments on the "inevitability" of elite rule as expressed above cast a heavy shadow on his work and call into question the accuracy of his observations. The "realistic science" that Mosca wanted to develop, writes Tom Bottomore, was in fact primarily intended to refute Marx's theory of class on two essential points:

> First, to show that the Marxist conception of a "ruling *class*" is erroneous, by demonstrating the continual circulation of elites, which prevents in most societies, and especially in modern industrial societies, the formation of a stable and closed ruling class; and secondly, to show that a classless society is impossible, since in every society there is, and must be, a minority which actually rules.[17]

"In the world in which we are living," Mosca wrote quite bluntly, "socialism will be arrested only if a realistic political science succeeds in demolishing the metaphysical and optimistic methods that prevail at present in social studies."[18] Targeting in particular Marx and his theory of historical materialism, Mosca argued that his book *The Ruling Class* "is a refutation of it."[19]

Although Mosca believed that the ruling classes throughout history "owe their special qualities not so much to the blood in their veins as to their very particular upbringing,"[20] and recognized that "social position, family tradition, the habits of the class in which we live, contribute more than is commonly supposed to the greater or lesser development of the qualities mentioned,"[21] he nonetheless failed to address the social implications of his own position by rejecting the class-struggle analysis of Marx and opting instead for a psychological theory of power based on an individualistic conception of human nature.

Bureaucratic Organization

Robert Michels (1876–1936), the third influential classical elite theorist, stressed that the source of the problem of elite rule lies in the nature and structure of bureaucratic organization.[22] He argued that the bureaucratic organization itself, irrespective of the intentions of bureaucrats, results in the formation of an elite-dominated society. Thus, regardless of ideological ends, organizational means would inevitably lead to oligarchic rule: "It is organization which gives birth to the domination of the elected over the electors, of the mandataries over the mandators, of the delegates over the delegators. Who says organization, says oligarchy."[23]

At the heart of Michels's theoretical model lie the three basic principles of elite formation that take place within the bureaucratic structure of political organization: (1) the need for specialized staff, facilities, and, above all, leaders; (2) the utilization of such specialized facilities by leaders within these organizations; and (3) the psychological attributes of the leaders (i.e., charisma).

Michels argued that the bureaucratic structure of modern political parties or organizations gives rise to specific conditions that corrupt the leaders and bureaucrats in such parties. These leaders, in turn, consolidate the power of the party leadership and set themselves apart from the masses. This is so, goes the argument, not only with the so-called democratic organizations of bourgeois society, but with socialist parties as well. Michels, a one-time "socialist," thought that if socialist parties, dedicated as they were to the highest egalitarian values, were undemocratic and elitist, then all organizations had to be elitist.

"Even the purest of idealists who attains to power for a few years," he wrote, "is unable to escape the corruption which the exercise of power carries in its train."[24] For Michels, this pointed to the conservative basis of (any) organization, since the *organizational form* as such was the basis of the conservatism, and this conservatism was the inevitable outcome of power attained through political organization. Hence, "political organization leads to power, but power is always conservative."[25]

Based on this reasoning, one might think that Michels was an anarchist; he was not. He insisted that any organization, *including those of the anarchists*, was subject to the "iron law":

> Anarchism, a movement on behalf of liberty, founded on the inalienable right of the human being over his own person, succumbs, no less than the Socialist Party, to the law of authoritarianism as soon as it abandons the region of pure thought and as soon as its adherents unite to form associations aiming at any sort of political activity.[26]

This same phenomenon of elitism/authoritarianism, argued Michels, also occurs at the individual level. Hence, to close the various gaps in his theory, Michels resorted to human-nature-based tautological arguments: Once a person ascends to the leadership level, he becomes a part of his new social milieu to the extent that he would resist ever leaving that position. The argument here is that the leader consolidates his power around the newly acquired condition and uses that power to serve his interests by perpetuating the maintenance of that power. In order to avoid this and eliminate authoritarianism, which comes about in "associations aiming at any sort of political activity," one must not "abandon the region of pure thought"! Herein lay the self-serving conservatism of Michels, who in the latter part of his life turned, like Pareto before him, to the cause of Italian fascism.

In his "Introduction" to a recent edition of Michels's book *Political Parties*, Seymour Martin Lipset writes:

> Michels, who had been barred from academic appointment in Germany for many years, . . . left his position at the University of Basle to accept a chair at the University of Perugia offered to him personally by Benito Mussolini in 1928.[27]

Lipset goes on to point out: "Michels found his charismatic leader in Benito Mussolini. For him, Il Duce translated 'in a naked and brilliant form the aims of the multitude.'"[28] Finally, Michels "died as a supporter of fascist rule in Italy."[29]

Conclusion

The three major proponents of elite theory—Pareto, Mosca, and Michels—have provided a political theory of elites that they believed explains the nature and dynamics of power in modern society. Best exemplified in Mosca's characterization of the ruling class as the governing elite of full-time politicians in charge of the state apparatus and society in general, classical elite theory has argued in favor of a theory based on a conceptualization centered in bureaucratic organization, particularly in the sphere of politics. Hence, in a manner different from Weber's characterization of bureaucracy, which he viewed as a tool *of* power lodged in the economic (market) sphere, classical elite theorists-especially Mosca and Michels—argue that power in society resides in government and the governing elite.

Given its contempt for the masses and its acceptance of elite rule over them as an inevitable outcome of bureaucratic organization prevalent in modern politics, classical elite theory lends itself to antipopular, reactionary conclusions that have important political implications that are quite different from Weber's formulation of the question and are diametrically opposite to that of Marx and Engels regarding the prospects for change and social transformation in society today.

Notes

1. Vilfredo Pareto, *The Mind and Society*, 4 vols., ed. Arthur Livingstone (New York: Harcourt, Brace, 1935).
2. Ibid., 3:1423.
3. Ibid., 1423–24; italics in the original.
4. Ibid., 1430–31.
5. Ibid., 1431.
6. Ibid.
7. Ibid., 1:40.
8. Ibid., 3:1430.
9. Ibid.
10. Irving M. Zeitlin, *Ideology and the Development of Sociological Theory* (Englewood Cliffs, N.J.: Prentice Hall, 1968), 194.
11. Ibid.
12. Gaetano Mosca, *The Ruling Class* (New York: McGraw-Hill, 1939), 50.
13. Ibid., 326.
14. Ibid., 51.
15. Ibid., 329.
16. Ibid., 329.
17. Tom Bottomore, *Elites and Society* (Baltimore, Md.: Penguin, 1966), 17–18.
18. Mosca, *The Ruling Class*, 327.
19. Ibid., 447.
20. Ibid., 62.
21. Ibid., 63.
22. Robert Michels, *Political Parties* (New York: Free Press, 1968).
23. Ibid., 365.
24. Ibid., 355.
25. Ibid., 333.
26. Ibid., 327–28.
27. Seymour Martin Lipset, "Introduction," in Michels, *Political Parties*, 33.
28. Ibid., 32.
29. Ibid., 38.

Chapter 5

COOLEY AND MEAD ON HUMAN NATURE AND SOCIETY*

In the closing decades of the nineteenth century and the opening decades of the twentieth, Charles Horton Cooley (1864–1929) and George Herbert Mead (1863–1931), along with the pragmatist John Dewey, represented the very best that the philosophical camp of social idealism had to offer. They helped found a major new variety of social psychological reasoning, which was later to be called symbolic interactionism. Their concern with the fate of the person caught up in the massive process of industrialization led them to focus on the relationship between the individual and the collectivity. Herein lies their contribution. This chapter therefore focuses on their views of "self" and "society."

Society and the Individual

From Cooley's perspective, "The imaginations which people have of one another are the solid facts of society."[1] Society lives in the minds of the members constituting the social unit, and this is precisely what makes the unit something very real as far as its members are concerned. Cooley equates mental and social life, but he also notes that society has a structure and that structure evinces the characteristics of a complex organism:

> [Society] is a complex of forms of processes each of which is living or growing by interaction with the others, the whole thing being so unified that what takes place in one part affects all the rest. It is a vast tissue of reciprocal activity, differentiated into innumerable systems, some of them quite distinct, others not readily traceable, and all interwoven to such a degree that you see different systems according to the point of view you take.[2]

*This chapter was written by Larry T. Reynolds.

Cooley obviously prefers to focus not on individuals but on society, but only as society is maintained in the imaginations or minds of individuals. He simultaneously avoided the overpowering social determinism of classic organicism and the instinct or propensity-driven model of extreme individualism. Given his conception of the nature of human collectivities, it is not difficult to see how Cooley reached the conclusion that the individual and society were but two sides of the same coin, which is to say, inseparable.

Cooley also developed a methodology compatible with his theories of self and society. If "the imaginations which people have of one another are the solid facts of society," it follows that in order to best understand social life one must somehow gain access to these "imaginations," which are not directly accessible when one simply observes external behavior. As these "imaginations," these "ideas," are, in a sense, accessible only to those that experience them, Cooley advocated a methodological strategy termed "sympathetic introspection." One is to place oneself in touch with society's members and sympathetically try to imagine life as these members live it. One seeks, then, to detail, describe, and understand the imagination of others, because these imaginations are the solid facts of society. One needs to imagine as others imagine.

Given Cooley's views on the nature of human society and how best to study it, he developed two concepts to facilitate the task: (1) the *primary group*, and (2) the *looking-glass self*. These two concepts dovetail nicely with his conception of society and also allow him to work out his view of human nature.

The Primary Group and the Looking-Glass Self

In looking at the "primary group" and the "looking-glass self," it must be kept in mind that for Cooley the concepts of group and self are dynamically intertwined. The self develops in a group context, and the primary group is the true seat of self-development. Primary groups are important for three reasons: (1) they are the building blocks for more complex social relationships, (2) they are the mechanisms through which the self evolves, and (3) they are the linkage points between the larger social order and its human elements, individuals. Cooley defines primary groups as follows:

> By primary groups I mean those characterized by intimate face-to-face association and co-operation. They are primary in several senses, but chiefly in that they are fundamental in forming the social nature of the ideas of individuals.[3]

From Cooley's vantage point, the self is developed and defined in the course of interaction with others; it is a social product produced, for the most part, in the primary group. This social product is best referred to as a "looking-glass self," in that the child obtains an identity only with the realization that a picture, idea, or image of oneself "reflects" other people's perceptions. What is reflected is the imaginations of others concerning the individual. In the mind of society's members, the self resides; it constitutes an imaginative act. The specific social reference for the self, argues Cooley,

> takes the form of a somewhat definite imagination of how one's self—that is, any idea he appropriates—appears in a particular mind, and the kind of self-feeling one has is determined by the attitude toward this attributed to the other mind. A social self of this sort might be called the reflected or looking-glass self.[4]

In simple terms, "We always imagine, and in imagining, share, the judgments of the other mind."[5] Charles Cooley's notion of the "looking-glass self" has three components: (1) our imagination of how we *appear* to others, (2) our imagination of how others *judge* our appearance, and (3) our resultant self-feelings, which are produced by such imaginings.

This conceptualization of self and the way it is formed has important consequences. Sheldon Stryker summarizes them as follows:

> there is and can be no individuality outside of the social order; individual personality is a 'natural' development from existing social life and the state of communications among the persons sharing that life; and, the expectations of others are central to this development.[6]

In the writings of Charles Horton Cooley, especially those on human nature, self, and society was food for future social psychological theory.

Mind, Self, and Society

As Mead sees it, the full range of truly human conduct unfolds only in the course of the association of actors with one another. Human life is, in essence, social life, group life. And social life is essentially a matter of cooperative behavior. According to Mead, humans cooperate because they have the ability to take the other's point of view—to mentally place themselves in the position of the other, and in so doing to take that "other's" point of view into account. In short, we are able to form a conception of the perspectives held by other persons. We can and do act in concert because we share common expectations both for our own behavior and that of others. Our more complex forms of social organization, such as social institutions and even society itself, mirror this same process. This is clearly seen in Mead's definition of social institutions:

> the institutions of society are organized forms of groups or social activity—forms so organized that the individual members of society can act adequately and socially by taking the attitudes of others toward these activities."[7]

With the understanding of others' behaviors that results from putting oneself in their place, the person structures her or his conduct in a manner that allows it to fit in with the behavior of others. In carrying on common action, group members influence themselves and others in a similar fashion. Mead puts this in the following terms:

> The very stimulus which one gives to another to carry out his part of the common act affects the individual who so affects the other in the same sense. He tends to arouse the same activity in himself which he arouses in the other.[8]

Among these stimuli which people present to others are "gestures." A *gesture* is a *portion of an act* that nevertheless *stands for the whole act*. When an individual makes a gesture (e.g., displays a clinched fist), the person who is the recipient of the gesture completes in her or his imagination the act that the gesture stands for. The recipient projects the gesture into the future: "I am going to get punched." The recipient understands the act stood for by the gesture; the gesture's meaning is taken. Happily, people have the ability to respond to their own gestures. Therefore, they can attach to their own gestures the same meaning that others attach to them; the individual can complete the act just as others complete it. When shared meanings attach to gestures, they become significant symbols.

A system of significant symbols, of linguistic elements, constitutes a language. Through the use of language, human society and the human individual communicate. Individuals, because they can respond to their own gestures, can share each other's experiences, can forge a common basis for organized social life, and in cooperation can establish a society. Human behavior is social in character, not only because we respond to the behavior of others but because the *behavior of others* is *incorporated in our own* behavior—and "ours" is incorporated in "theirs." According to Mead, we can respond to ourselves as others respond to us, and because we do, we imaginatively share the behavior of our fellow citizens. Our relationship with others is a product of our ability to respond to our own gestures and imaginatively to place ourselves in the position of others:

> We are more or less seeing ourselves as others see us. We are unconsciously addressing ourselves as others address us. . . . We are calling out in the other person something we are calling out in ourselves, so that unconsciously we take over these attitudes. We are unconsciously putting ourselves in the place of others and acting as others act.[9]

Thus is human society possible, and this society is the source of the social genesis of both selfs and minds.

The Self

From Mead's perspective, the most important thing about human society is that it is made up of persons with selves. If you are capable of acting toward yourself as you act toward others, then you have a self. To possess a self means that you can respond to yourself as an object. It means that you have the capacity of gaining perspective on yourself by looking back as others would look on you.

The existence of human society necessarily implies the existence of role taking; role taking, in turn, is the underlying mechanism producing the self. Through the process of role taking, the individual becomes capable of treating oneself as an object, becomes capable of gaining and maintaining "social distance" from oneself. The self develops during childhood, and childhood activity plays an instrumental role in that development because through initial attempts at role taking, the child begins to gain a modicum of social distance from oneself. This takes place through the three stages described below.

The first stage can be labeled the *imitation* or *preparatory* stage, and during this stage the child begins, through the process of meaningless imitation, to gain a small amount of social distance from oneself. Lacking any real comprehension of what he or she is doing, the child imitates, or does, things that others around are doing. A two-year old girl pretending to read a magazine with her father is starting to extricate herself from herself. She is engaging in the initial process of role taking: she is incipiently placing herself in the position of her father and "acting" like him.

In the second, *play* stage, the child gains additional distance from self by exaggerating the imitation process. The child in sequential fashion pretends to be several different people. Actual role playing is starting to take place. As the child is here directing activity toward itself by taking the roles of others, a self is now being formed. Evidence of this self-formation presents itself when the child refers to herself in such terms as "Scarlet is sleepy" or "Scarlet is a good girl." The child is now not only seeing oneself from the perspective of others, but is actually beginning to "take on" these perspectives as one's own. During the play stage, the child has yet to develop a consistent, or uniform, vantage point from which to view oneself.

During the final, or *game*, stage, the child develops the ability to simultaneously take a number of roles. Several other persons' expectations must be simultaneously responded to. The child can now respond to what Mead called "the generalized other." He or she now sees the community of interests as over and against the interests of any one other. Children can now view themselves from the perspective of the group, community, or even society as a whole. Once a child has taken on this generalized standpoint, it becomes possible to conduct oneself in a consistent, organized fashion. The self can be viewed from a consistent standpoint. The game stage is the completing stage of the self, but while the self is a process that develops in stages, it is a process that has its own definite elements, or structures.

While the self is best conceptualized as a social process within the individual, it involves two "distinguishable phases," called respectively the "I" and the "me".[10] The impulsive and spontaneous tendencies of the actor are represented by the "I"; it is the unpredictable, unorganized, uncertain, and undirected component in human experience. It is the spontaneous spark of energy within the individual. The "I" is a manifestation of both natural needs and impulses, it is a process of thinking as well as acting, and, because it represents the unpredictable and spontaneous, its presence means that human beings will never be the completely passive agents, mere reflections of the larger social order, that conservative theorists are pleased to see them as being.

The "me" is the phase of the self that represents the group's common meanings, definitions, expectations, values, and understandings. Depending on the situation, the "me" may comprise a specific other or the generalized other. It represents the incorporated other(s) within the individual.[11]

Human acts start in the form of the "I" and tend to terminate in the form of the "me". However, while the "me" establishes limits within which the "I" must act, if "the stress becomes too great, these limits are not observed, and an individual asserts himself in perhaps a violent fashion." When this happens "the 'I' is the dominant element over and against the 'me'."[12] Typically, the "me" provides direction to an ongoing act, while its initial propulsion comes from the "I". The act is a product of the dynamic interplay between the two phases of the self. Conformity appends to the "me" and novelty to the "I"; the "me" represents society's influence on the individual and the "I" the person's impact on society. It is in the give and take between the "I" and "me" phases of self that novel experience becomes possible, while social control becomes, at least partly, "self control."

The Mind

As Mead has pointed out, "the origin of minds and the interaction among minds become mysteries" if one assumes the existence of individual minds and then attempts to derive social life and processes from them. He rejects such an approach and, as he did with respect to the self, argues instead that *mind* is a *social product*: "Mind arises through communication by a conversation of gestures in a social process or context of experience."[13] It is through communication by means of significant symbols that mind arises, and the mind is present when the person employs such symbols in interacting with oneself. The gestures and significant symbols pointed to by Mead are extremely important; only by means of them can thinking take place.

Mead's analysis of mind starts with a consideration of the relationship of the person to her or his environment. The relationship of the individual to the environment is one of adaptation. People, in a sense, determine which aspects of the environment they are going to pay attention to, but their selective reaction to the environment is not automatic. There is typically a hesitancy before overt action, and *when overt behavior is inhibited*, when one is mentally contemplating alternative courses of subsequent action, *when one is assessing* the future *consequences* of present *behavior* in terms of past experience, then *mind is present*.

Minded behavior, or thinking, arises in the face of problems, in the light of the blockage of the act, or as Mead put it "All analytic thought commences with the presence of problems."[14] Minded behavior is simply contemplating in the light of previous experience the possible consequences of different lines of future conduct before selecting the one alternative to be acted on. Past, present, and future all come together in this process called mind. This process of minded behavior dictates that humans construct their acts in the course of their responses to their environments.

Mead pointed out that people respond to what he called "objects." Objects are plans of action; people perceive things in terms of experiences one would have if a plan of action were carried out toward that object. One sees objects in terms of the use to be made of them or the action to be directed toward them. Objects exist only when we indicate them to ourselves. To indicate something to oneself is to take others into account. As "others' definitions" are implicated in our indicating objects to ourselves, objects are largely shared, or social, objects. Hence, while we indeed select those objects which make up our social habitats, we do so on a social as well as an individual basis.

Cooperative social activity forms the matrix out of which communication arises, and such communication is, in turn, the very process out of which mind arises. During the course of interacting with others, some initial gestures of the human infant are favorably received. Soon certain gestures come to have common meanings for both the child and her or his associates. Such consensually agreed upon gestures Mead calls "conventional gestures." Through these conventional gestures and additional linguistic symbols, the child learns the "meanings," or definitions, of the collectivity to which he or she belongs, learns to take the role of others, and comes to possess the ability to think. A socially generated mind not only enables the individual to adjust to society but, in turn, makes possible society's continued existence.

George Herbert Mead's working conceptualization of mind, self, and society furthered the development of social psychological theorizing in the United States.

Conclusion

Charles Horton Cooley and George Herbert Mead played a key role in shaping the most sophisticated variety of social behaviorism currently found in American sociology, the social psychological framework known as symbolic interactionism. Their strong emphasis on the group, especially the "primary group," as the basic molder of individual behavior and the "real place" one has to first look in order to explain such conduct became a cornerstone in social psychological theory. Their concepts the "looking-glass self" and the "social self" impact heavily on contemporary treatments of personality. Their views on the importance of gestures, symbols, and language in shaping behavior and integrating society are still in force among sociologists and social psychologists alike. Both Cooley and Mead favored those methodological techniques, strategies, and devices which are today called "qualitative approaches," and which find favor among a growing number of sociologists.

While the approach represented by Cooley and Mead has its shortcomings—e.g., it is fairly ahistorical and needs to provide a better analysis of large-scale societal structures—one real measure of their success stands out in that many of their insights are taken for granted by today's social psychologists.

Notes

1. Charles Horton Cooley, *Human Nature and Social Order* (New York: Scribner's, 1902), 87.
2. Cooley, *Social Process* (New York: Scribner's, 1918), 28.
3. Cooley, *Social Organization* (New York: Scribner's, 1909), 23.
4. Cooley, *Human Nature and Social Order*, 151–152.
5. Ibid., 152–153.
6. Sheldon Stryker, *Symbolic Interactionism* (Menlo Park, Calif.: Benjamin Cummings, 1980), 29.
7. George Herbert Mead, *Mind. Self and Society: From the Standpoint of a Social Behaviorist*, edited by Charles Morris (Chicago: University of Chicago Press, 1934), 261.

8. Ibid., 137.
9. Ibid., 68–69.
10. Ibid., 178.
11. Bernard N. Meltzer, *The Social Psychology of George Herbert Mead* (Kalamazoo, Mich.: Western Michigan University Center for Sociological Research, 1964), 17.
12. Mead, *Mind, Self and Society*, 210.
13. Ibid., 55.
14. George Herbert Mead, "Suggestions Toward a Theory of Philosophical Disciplines," *Philosophical Review* 9 (1900), 2.1.

Chapter 6

FREUD ON THE DEVELOPMENT OF SOCIETY AND CIVILIZATION

The controversies surrounding the development of a psychoanalytic theory of society earlier in this century have given rise to a number of critical approaches to Freudian psychology.[1] Some controversial figures, such as Wilhelm Reich, have attempted to develop a Marx-Freud synthesis to explore the political sources of mass psychology and explain the rise of fascism in Germany.[2] Others, such as Erich Fromm and Herbert Marcuse, have developed their own distinct versions of this synthesis, focusing on the cultural, ideological, and philosophical dimensions of Freudian theory that informs a critical analysis of modern society.[3]

This chapter examines Sigmund Freud's concept of human nature, the origins and development of society and civilization, and the nature of religion, so that we can better evaluate the significance of such syntheses and the extent and depth of Freud's contribution to classical social theory.

Human Nature and Character Structure

Sigmund Freud (1856–1939) viewed the individual as an organism driven by an instinctual energy called libido. Contrary to the arguments of some who have set forth a narrow, vulgar interpretation of libido as purely a sexual drive, others have maintained that the Freudian libidinal instinct

> is manifested not only in childhood sexuality, attachment to parents and brotherly love, but in art, work, aggression and just about all forms of human behavior involving emotional commitment including the feelings associated with the concepts "self-respect," "human dignity," "fraternity" and "equality."[4]

Moreover, Freud's broader characterization of libido as a more generalized drive for human satisfaction can be deduced from his observation suggesting that creative work may provide a primary release for libidinal energies:

> The possibility [work] offers of displacing a large amount of libidinal components, whether narcissistic, aggressive or even erotic, on to professional work and on to the human relations connected with it lends it a value by no means second to what it enjoys as something indispensible to the preservation and justification of existence in society. Professional activity is a source of special satisfaction if it is a freely chosen one—if, that is to say, by means of sublimation, it makes possible the use of existing inclinations, of persisting or constitutionally reinforced instinctual impulses.[5]

Focusing on the inner workings of human behavior, Freud concludes that there exists two contradictory processes: "After long doubts and vacillations," he writes, "we have decided to assume the existence of only two basic instincts, Eros and the destructive instinct."[6]

> The aim of the first of these basic instincts is to establish ever greater unities and to preserve them thus—in short, to bind together; the aim of the second, on the contrary, is to undo connections and so to destroy things. We may suppose that the final aim of the destructive instinct is to reduce living things to an inorganic state. For this reason we also call it the *death instinct*. . . .
>
> In biological functions the two basic instincts work against each other or combine with each other.[7]

These basic instincts, Freud tells us, represent "forces which we assume to exist behind the tensions caused by the needs of the id."[8] Furthermore, "they represent the somatic demands upon mental life. . . . [T]hey are the ultimate cause of all activity."[9]

These instincts, then, lie at the very core of human personality or character structure, and it is through the dynamic parts or mechanisms of this structure that one relates to others and to the external world. The three component parts of the individual's character structure, in the Freudian model, are the "id," the "ego," and the "superego"; together, they form the topography of the mind.

"The power of the id," Freud asserts, "expresses the true purpose of the individual organism's life. This consists in the satisfaction of its innate needs."[10]

> In the id there are no conflicts; contradictions and antitheses exist side by side, and often equalize matters between themselves by compromise formations. . . .
>
> [E]verything which goes on in the id is unconscious and remains so.[11]

Consequently,

> the core of our being, then, is formed by the obscure id, which has no direct relations with the external world and is accessible even to our own knowledge only through the medium of another agency of the mind. . . .
>
> The id, which is cut off from the external world, has its own world perception.[12]

In short, according to Freud, the id is our instinctual nature; it represents the drive for the satisfaction of our innate needs.

The ego, in contrast, is the organized part of the id. It mediates the demands of the id, on the one hand, and that of the realities of the external world as well as the superego, on the other. In Freud's words:

> the ego is in control of voluntary movement. It has the task of self-preservation. As regards *external* events, it performs that task by becoming aware of the stimuli from without. . . . As regards *internal* events, in relation to the id, it performs that task by gaining control over the demands of the instincts, by deciding whether they shall be allowed to obtain satisfaction, by postponing that satisfaction to times and circumstances favorable in the external world or by suppressing their excitations completely.[13]

Finally, the super-ego, according to Freud, is the conscience of internalized prohibitions of our culture. To the extent that these prohibitions imposed on individuals by society or civilization come to repress and frustrate libidinal energies, aggression is the result. If such aggression is not channeled through some social mechanism to release it, then the individual can become neurotic. Otherwise, the collective yearning to release repressed libidinal energies may trigger a social response that might have revolutionary political implications!

The Origins and Development of Society and Civilization

Society and civilization, in Freudian theory, have their roots in the material conditions of human social existence. Hence, for Freud, the rise and development of human societies must be explained through a concrete analysis of the social world. "Human civilization," Freud explains,

> includes on the one hand all the knowledge and capacity that men have acquired in order to control the forces of nature and extract its

> wealth for the satisfaction of human needs, and, on the other hand, all the regulations necessary in order to adjust the relations of men to one another and especially the distribution of the available wealth. The two trends of civilization are not independent of each other.[14]

The development of civilization, Freud argues, is thus the result of the physiological imperatives of survival (i.e., food, shelter, and physical security) and the society's need to organize social relations to maintain social order. "If we go back far enough," Freud writes, "we find that the first acts of civilization were the use of tools, the gaining of control over fire and the construction of dwellings."[15] At a certain point in history, humans realized that it would be to their advantage to work in cooperation with others to overcome the immense difficulties posed by nature, which threatened human survival. This cooperative work among individuals led to the formation of groups that were mutually beneficial for all. In Freud's words:

> After primal man had discovered that it lay in his own hands, literally, to improve his lot on earth by working, it cannot have been a matter of indifference to him whether another man worked with or against him. The other man acquired the value for him of a fellow-worker, with whom it was useful to live together. Even earlier, in his ape-like prehistory, man had adopted the habit of forming families, and the members of his family were probably his first helpers.[16]

For Freud, then, civilization is rooted in an individual's relationship with nature and with other individuals—in developing the necessary technology to sustain life and in satisfying his or her social needs. Thus, Freud gives us a materialist analysis of the rise and development of society and civilization. He argues that the human group has its roots in the material conditions of its social existence in nature and that the mechanism that facilitates this process is the family.

The family, through the social relationships it engages in, channels instinctual energies and forms the child's character structure. Through this process the family thus becomes the mechanism that produces and socializes children who are fitted to the social roles that society requires them to fulfill. In this way the family comes to play a key role in rationalizing and reinforcing the existing social order.[17]

The role of the family in facilitating the preservation of the modern social order is a central one in the Freudian view, as the social and class structure of society is transmitted to future generations through the socialization process that develops and matures in the family. Thus, "the social relationships of the family . . . channels instinctual energies and forms the child's character structure."[18] And with the development of this character structure, the family passes on to future generations the socially accepted roles that one's offspring acquire.

The recognition by some Marxist theorists of the process surrounding the role of the family in facilitating the maintenance of the status quo led to the development of the Marx-Freud synthesis in the earlier part of this century. The proponents of this approach developed their analysis to examine the reasons for the prevalence of false consciousness among the working class and see how it can be transformed into class consciousness that the working class family could promote to advance its class interests.

A recent proponent of this approach, Albert Szymanski, points out that, in his analysis of the family, Freud

> mistakenly assumes the logic of the family triad to be universal among "civilized" homo sapiens. The early synthesizers of Marx and Freud, on the other hand, put the family in historical context, recognizing Freud's universal family for the bourgeois family it is. They understood that families in different societies and different classes would have different logics and consequently would produce different typical character structures.[19]

To maintain their control over society, the dominant classes, through the institutions they control—which in turn have great influence on the family—channel behavior to conform to the values promoted by the existing social order. Thus, the development of a character structure that conforms to the prevailing status quo

> results in passive and dependent people who have internalized the necessities of class society and the capital accumulation process. Political conservatism among the masses of the oppressed thus becomes firmly rooted. False-consciousness among people who should be among the most active supporters of revolution is securely anchored by these mechanisms in the very psychology of the oppressed.[20]

Moreover:

> Conservatism and reaction in all its forms—religion, nationalism, fascism, etc.—on the one hand ward off rational impulses [to freedom, dignity and self-determination] and on the other offer substitute gratifications in aggressive behavior towards other "races" and nations or against the very groups and individuals

> which advocate liberation. Racism, fascism and extreme nationalism are thus firmly rooted in the character structures of large segments of the oppressed. These phenomena are consequently far more than mere attitudes, values, norms, or prejudices; they are based in the organization of our psychic energies.[21]

Thus, in order to eliminate these phenomena, which block the development of class consciousness, one "must remove the source of the energy behind such behavior, not just 'reeducate,' i.e., the libidinal repression necessitated by the logic of capitalism must be eliminated by destroying that logic itself."[22]

Religion

Religion and religious ideas, for Freud, are likewise the manifestations of material conditions in social life; they reflect the basic social organization of society. Hence religious phenomena, Freud argues, must be explained from the standpoint of a materialist understanding of social reality-one that locates religion within the confines of existing society.

Perhaps one of the clearest statements of Freud's social conception of religion can be found in the following passage:

> Religion . . . is an attempt to get control over the sensory world, in which we are placed, by means of the wish world which we have developed inside us as a result of biological and psychological necessities. But it cannot achieve its end. Its doctrines carry with them the stamp of the times in which they originate, the ignorant childhood days of the human race.[23]

Arguing that religion plays an illusory role and mystifies the nature of human relations in society, Freud proclaims the abolition of religion as the first step toward the demystification of social reality, hence clearing the way for the realization of true human potential. In his dialogue with his imaginary opponent in *The Future of an Illusion*, Freud argues that "religious doctrines . . . should cease to be put forward as the reasons for the precepts of civilization."[24] Moreover, "those historical residues," he adds,

> have helped us to view religious teachings, as it were, as neurotic relics, and we may now argue that the time has probably come, as it does in an analytic treatment, for replacing the effects of repression by the results of the rational operation of the intellect. We may foresee, but hardly regret, that such a process of remolding

> will not stop at renouncing the solemn transfiguration of cultural percepts, but that a general revision of them will result in many of them being done away with.[25]

"[R]eligious doctrines will have to be discarded," Freud insists,

> no matter whether the first attempts fail, or whether the first substitutes prove to be untenable. . . . [I]n the long run nothing can withstand reason and experience, and the contradiction which religion offers to both is all too palpable.[26]

Through the abolition of religion, then, humanity will be able to free itself from illusions and actively intervene in history to liberate itself from repression and move toward the satisfaction of truly human needs—needs that precisely form the very core of the human experience.

Conclusion

The above analysis of the Freudian approach in classical social theory reveals a number of strands in the application of psychoanalytic theory to explain social reality. We have argued that once they are stripped of their biological connotations, Freud's arguments in essence are socially based and represent the inner workings of social life that he was able to express through his materialist analysis of society and the social order within which the individual is situated. Thus, for Freud, the discontented individual becomes stressed because society limits individual freedoms by repressing his or her innate psychological drives. Further, the major institutions of society—such as the family, the state, and religion—play a pivotal role in perpetuating this condition to maintain social order. From a dialectical standpoint, however, these very same institutions can also become key instruments of change that help *transform* society and achieve genuine freedom for the individual and the social collectivity as a whole.

The significance of the Freudian model, then, is such that, if interpreted within its social and material context, it can add an important dimension to sociological analysis and make a significant contribution to the body of knowledge that represents the best in classical social theory.

Notes

1. For a critical analysis of the origins and development of psychoanalysis in the United States, see Harry K. Wells, *The Failure of Psychoanalysis* (New York: International Publishers, 1963); and C.P. Oberndorf, *A History of Psychoanalysis in America* (New York: Grune, 1953). See also Martin Jay, *The Dialectical Imagination* (Boston: Little Brown, 1973), chap. 3.

2. See, for example, Wilhelm Reich, *Character Analysis* (New York: Orgone Institute Press, 1949); idem, *The Mass Psychology of Fascism* (New York: Farrar, Strauss and Giroux, 1970); and idem, *Sex Pol: Essays, 1929–1934* (New York: Random House, 1972).

3. For a sampling of Fromm's writings, see Erich Fromm, *Beyond the Chains of Illusion* (New York: Simon and Schuster, 1962); and idem, *The Crisis of Psychoanalysis* (New York: Holt, Rinehart, Winston, 1970). For some of Marcuse's most influential works, see Herbert Marcuse, *One Dimensional Man* (Boston: Beacon Press, 1964); and idem, *Eros and Civilization* (New York: Vintage Books, 1968).

4. Al Szymanski, "The Revolutionary Uses of Freudian Theory," *Social Praxis* 5, nos. 1–2 (1976): 46.

5. Sigmund Freud, *Civilization and Its Discontents* (New York: Norton, 1962), 27.

6. Sigmund Freud, *An Outline of Psychoanalysis* (New York: Norton, 1949), 20.

7. Ibid., 20–21.

8. Ibid., 19.

9. Ibid.

10. Ibid.

11. Sigmund Freud, *The Question of Lay Analysis* (New York: Norton, 1950), 36, 38.

12. Freud, *An Outline of Psychoanalysis*, 108–9.

13. Ibid., 15–16.

14. Sigmund Freud, *The Future of an Illusion* (Garden City, NY: Anchor, 1961), 2–3.

15. Freud, *Civilization and Its Discontents*, 37.

16. Ibid., 46.

17. Szymanski, "The Revolutionary Uses of Freudian Theory," 32.

18. Ibid., 30.

19. Ibid.

20. Ibid., 36.

21. Ibid.

22. Ibid.

23. Sigmund Freud, *New Introductory Lectures on Psychoanalysis*, 168.

24. Freud, *The Future of an Illusion*, 72.

25. Ibid., 72–73.

26. Ibid., 88–89.

Chapter 7

GRAMSCI AND LENIN ON IDEOLOGY, THE STATE, AND REVOLUTION

While the classical elite theorists held the masses in contempt and sided with the ruling classes as the engines of social development, V.I. Lenin (1870–1924) and Antonio Gramsci (1891–1937), like Marx and Engels before them, threw in their lot with the laboring masses and saw the working class as the leading revolutionary force to transform capitalist society.

This chapter takes a brief look at the central arguments of Gramsci and Lenin on the nature and role of the state and ideological hegemony and explores the underlying class contradictions of capitalist society which, they argued, would lead to its revolutionary transformation.

Class Struggle and the State

Outlined in its clearest and most concise form in his classic work *The State and Revolution*, Lenin explains that in all class societies, the *class essence* of the state's rule over society is rooted in domination and exploitation by a propertied ruling class of the propertyless oppressed class.

In our epoch, writes Lenin, "every state in which private ownership of the land and means of production exists, in which capital dominates, however democratic it may be, is a capitalist state, a machine used by the capitalists to keep the working class and the poor peasants in subjection."[1]

Democracy in capitalist society, Lenin points out, is always bound by "the narrow limits set by capitalist exploitation, and consequently always remains, in effect, a democracy for the minority, only for the propertied classes, only for the rich."[2]

> Freedom in capitalist society always remains about the same as it was in the ancient Greek republics: freedom for the slave-owners. Owing to the conditions of capitalist exploitation, the modern wage slaves are so crushed by want and poverty that "they cannot

> be bothered with democracy," "cannot be bothered with politics"; in the ordinary, peaceful course of events, the majority of the population is debarred from participation in public and political life. . . .
>
> Democracy for an insignificant minority, democracy for the rich—that is the democracy of capitalist society. . . .
>
> Marx grasped this *essence* of capitalist democracy splendidly when, in analyzing the experience of the Commune, he said that the oppressed are allowed once every few years to decide which particular representatives of the oppressing class shall represent and repress them in parliament![3]

"People always have been the foolish victims of deception and self-deception in politics," Lenin continues elsewhere, "and they always will be until they have learnt to seek out the *interests* of some class or other behind all moral, religious, political and social phrases, declarations and promises."[4]

In class society, Lenin points out, the state has always been "an organ or instrument of violence exercised by one class against another."[5] And in capitalist society, this violence is exercised by the capitalist class against the working class. In an important passage in *The State and Revolution*, Lenin stresses that the state in capitalist society is not only the political organ of the capitalist class; it is structured in such a way that it guarantees the class rule of the capitalists and, short of a revolutionary rupture, its entrenched power is practically unshakable:

> A democratic republic is the best possible political shell for capitalism, and, therefore, once capital has gained possession of this very best shell . . . it establishes its power so securely, so firmly, that no change of persons, institutions or parties in the bourgeois-democratic republic can shake it.[6]

The question remains: With the obvious contradictions and conflicts between labor and capital, and with the evermore visible unity of capital and the state, how is capital able to convince broad segments of the laboring masses of the legitimacy of its class rule and the rule of the capitalist state over society?

Ideological Hegemony

In explaining the process by which the capitalist class disseminates its ideology through control of the state and its dominance over society, Antonio Gramsci drew attention to the ideological apparatuses of the capitalist state and introduced the concept of bourgeois cultural and ideological *hegemony*.[7] He stressed that it is not enough for the capitalist class simply to take control of the state machine and rule society directly through force and coercion; it must also convince the oppressed classes of the legitimacy of its rule: "The state is the entire complex of practical and theoretical activities with which the ruling class not only justifies and maintains its dominance, but manages to win the active consent of those over whom it rules."[8] Through its dominance of the superstructural organs of the state, the ruling class controls and shapes the ideas, hence consciousness, of the masses. Thus:

> Hegemony involves the successful attempts of the dominant class to use its political, moral, and intellectual leadership to establish its view of the world as all-inclusive and universal, and to shape the interests and needs of subordinate groups.[9]

With the acceptance of its ideas and the legitimization of its rule, the capitalist class is able to exercise control and domination of society through its ideological hegemony at the level of the superstructure with the aid and instrumentality of the state. Gramsci, writes Martin Carnoy, "assigned to the State part of this function of promoting a single (bourgeois) concept of reality, and, therefore, gave the State a more extensive (enlarged) role in perpetuating class,"[10] hence preventing the development of working-class consciousness. As such,

> it was not merely lack of understanding of their position in the economic process that kept workers from comprehending their class role, nor was it only the "private" institutions of society, such as religion, that were responsible for keeping the working class from self-realization, but it was the *State itself* that was involved in reproducing the relations of production. In other words, the State was much more than the coercive apparatus of the bourgeoisie; the State included the hegemony of the bourgeoisie in the superstructure.[11]

Although the dialectics of the accumulation process, which involves first and foremost the exploitation of labor, ultimately results in class struggle, civil war, and revolution to seize state power, the *ideological hegemony* of the ruling class, operating through the state itself, prolongs bourgeois class rule and institutionalizes and legitimizes exploitation. Gramsci argued that "the system's real strength does not lie in the violence of the ruling class or the coercive power of its state apparatus, but in the acceptance by the ruled of a 'conception of the world' which belongs to the rulers."[12] "False consciousness"—or lack of working-class consciousness and adoption of bourgeois ideas by the laboring masses—Gramsci argued, was the result of a complex process of bourgeois ideological hegemony that, operating through the superstructural (i.e., cultural, ideological, religious, and political) institutions of capitalist society, above all the bourgeois state, came to obtain the consent of the masses in convincing them of the correctness and superiority of the bourgeois worldview.

> In his doctrine of "hegemony," Gramsci saw that the dominant class did not have to rely solely on the coercive power of the State or even its direct economic power to rule; rather, through its hegemony, expressed in the civil society and the State, the ruled could be persuaded to accept the system of beliefs of the ruling class and to share its social, cultural, and moral values.[13]

"The philosophy of the ruling class," writes Giuseppe Fiori, "passes through a whole tissue of complex vulgarizations to emerge as 'common sense': that is, the philosophy of the masses, who accept the morality, the customs, the institutionalized behavior of the society they live in."[14] "The problem for Gramsci then," Fiori continues, "is to understand *how* the ruling class has managed to win the consent of the subordinate classes in this way; and then, to see how the latter will manage to overthrow the old order and bring about a new one of universal freedom."[15]

The increasing awareness of the working class of this process, hence the development of working-class consciousness, stresses Gramsci, helps expand the emerging class struggle from the economic and social spheres into the sphere of politics and ideology, so the struggle against capitalist ideology promoted by the bourgeois state and other ruling-class institutions becomes just as important, perhaps more so, as the struggle against capital develops and matures in other spheres of society. Countering the ideological hegemony of the capitalist class through the active participation of workers in their own collective organizations, the class-conscious organs of workers' power-militant trade unions, workers' political parties, and so forth—come to play a decisive role in gaining the political support of the laboring masses. In turn, through their newly gained awareness of their own class interests, the workers transcend the bounds of bourgeois ideological hegemony and develop their own counter (proletarian) political outlook—a process that accelerates with the further development of proletarian class consciousness. Thus, as the struggle against the state becomes an important part of the class struggle in general, the struggle against capitalism takes on a truly *political* and *ideological* content.

Gramsci's contribution to the Marxist theory of the state and of bourgeois ideological hegemony, then, both affirms *and* extends the analyses of the Marxist classics and advances our understanding of the processes of ruling-class domination and hegemony and the responses needed for the transformation of capitalist society.

The State and Revolution

Writing in August 1917, on the eve of the Great October Socialist Revolution in Russia, Lenin pointed out both the class nature of the state and, more important, the necessity of its revolutionary overthrow:

> If the state is the product of the irreconcilability of class antagonisms, if it is a power standing *above* society and "*alienating* itself *more and more* from it," it is clear that the liberation of the oppressed class is impossible not only without a violent revolution, *but also without the destruction* of the apparatus of state power which was created by the ruling class and which is the embodiment of this "alienation."[16]

Thus, for Lenin the transformation of capitalist society involves a revolutionary process in which a class-conscious working class, led by a disciplined workers' party, comes to adopt a radical solution to its continued exploitation and oppression under the yoke of capital and exerts its organized political force in a revolutionary rupture to take state power.

The victory of the working class in this struggle for power and control over society leads to the establishment of a socialist workers' state. The socialist state constitutes a new kind of state ruled by the working class and the laboring masses. The cornerstone of a workers' state, emerging out of capitalism, is the abolition of private property in the major means of production and an end to the exploitation of labor for private profit.

The establishment of a revolutionary dictatorship of the proletariat (as against the dictatorship of capital) is what distinguishes the socialist state from its capitalist counterpart. As the class essence of the state lies at the heart of an analysis of the nature and role of the state in different epochs throughout history, the class nature of the socialist state gives us clues to the nature and role of the state in a socialist society developing toward communism. For, as Marx has pointed out in *Critique of the Gotha Program*, the dictatorship of the proletariat (i.e., the class rule of the working class) is a transitional phase between capitalism and communism:

> Between capitalist and communist society lies the period of the revolutionary transformation of the one into the other. Corresponding to this is also a political transition period in which the state can be nothing but *the revolutionary dictatorship of the proletariat*.[17]

During this period, the state represents and defends the interests of the working class against capital and all other vestiges of reactionary exploitative classes, which, overthrown and dislodged from power, attempt in a multitude of ways to recapture the state through a counterrevolution.

"The theory of the class struggle, applied by Marx to the question of the state and the socialist revolution," writes Lenin,

> leads as a matter of course to the recognition of the *political rule* of the proletariat, of its dictatorship, i.e., of undivided power directly backed by the armed force of the people. The overthrow of the bourgeoisie can be achieved only by the proletariat becoming the *ruling class*, capable of crushing the inevitable and desperate resistance of the bourgeoisie, and of organizing all the working and exploited people for the new economic system.[18]

In this context, then, the proletarian state has a dual role to play: (1) to break the resistance of its class enemies (the exploiting classes); and (2) to protect the revolution and begin the process of socialist construction.

The Withering Away of the State

The class character of the new state under the dictatorship of the proletariat takes on a new form and content, according to Lenin: "During this period the state must inevitably be a state that is democratic *in a new way* (for the proletariat and the propertyless in general) and dictatorial *in a new way* (against the bourgeoisie)."[19] Thus,

> *simultaneously* with an immense expansion of democracy, which *for the first time* becomes democracy for the poor, democracy for the people, and not democracy for the money-bags, the dictatorship of the proletariat imposes a series of restrictions on the freedom of the oppressors, the exploiters, the capitalists.[20]

Used primarily to suppress these forces and build the material base of a classless, egalitarian society, the socialist state begins to wither away once there is no longer any need for it. As Engels points out:

> The first act in which the state really comes forward as the representative of society as a whole—the taking possession of the means of production in the name of society—is at the same time its last independent act as a state. The interference of the state power

> in social relations becomes superfluous in one sphere after another, and then ceases of itself. The government of persons is replaced by the administration of things and the direction of the processes of production. The state is not "abolished," *it withers away*.[21]

In this sense, the state no longer exists in the fully matured communist stage, for there is no longer the need in a classless society for an institution that is, by definition, an instrument of class rule through force and violence. Lenin writes:

> Only in communist society, when the resistance of the capitalists has been completely crushed, when the capitalists have disappeared, when there are no classes (i.e., when there is no distinctions between the members of society as regards their relation to the social means of production), only then "the state . . . ceases to exist," and "*it becomes possible to speak of freedom*." Only then will a truly complete democracy become possible and be realized, a democracy without any exceptions whatever.[22]

It is in this broader, transitional context that the class nature and tasks of the state in socialist society must be understood and evaluated, according to Lenin.

Thus, Lenin characterized the period of transition to communist society as exhibiting an infinitely higher form of democracy than that found in capitalist society, for democracy under socialism, he argued, is democracy for the masses, democracy for the great majority of the laboring population working together to build an egalitarian, classless society.

Notes

1. V.I. Lenin, *The State*, in Karl Marx, Frederick Engels, and V.I. Lenin, *On Historical Materialism* (New York: International Publishers, 1974), 641.
2. V.I. Lenin, *The State and Revolution*, in V.I. Lenin, *Selected Works in Three Volumes* (Moscow: Progress Publishers, 1975), 2:301.
3. Ibid., 301–2.
4. V.I. Lenin, "The Three Sources and Three Component Parts of Marxism," in V.I. Lenin, *Selected Works in One Volume* (New York: International Publishers, 1971), 24.
5. Lenin, *The State and Revolution*, 374.
6. Ibid., 247.
7. By *hegemony*, Gramsci meant the ideological predominance of the dominant ruling class(es) over the subordinate. At the same time, and in response to this, he introduced the concept of counterhegemony, which occurs when the proletariat, with the aid of "organic" intellectuals, exerts hegemony and exercises its superiority over society through the establishment of a proletarian socialist state.
8. Antonio Gramsci, *Prison Notebooks* (New York: International Publishers, 1971), 244.
9. Martin Carnoy, *The State and Political Theory* (Princeton: Princeton University Press, 1984), 70.

10. Ibid., 66.

11. Ibid.; emphasis in the original.

12. Giuseppe Fiori, *Antonio Gramsci, Life Revolutionary* (London: New Left Books, 1970), 238.

13. Carnoy, *The State and Political Theory*, 87.

14. Fiori, *Antonio Gramsci*, 238.

15. Ibid.

16. Lenin, *The State and Revolution*, 242; emphasis in the original.

17. Karl Marx, *Critique of the Gotha Programme*, in Karl Marx and Frederick Engels, *Selected Works* (New York: International Publishers, 1972), 331; emphasis in the original. For an extended discussion on the concept of the "dictatorship of the proletariat," see Etienne Balibar, *On the Dictatorship of the Proletaria*t (London: NLB, 1977).

18. Lenin, *The State and Revolution*, 255; emphasis in the original.

19. Ibid., 262; emphasis in the original.

20. Ibid., 302; emphasis in the original.

21. F. Engels, *Anti-Duhring* (New York: International Publishers, 1976), 307.

22. Lenin, *The State and Revolution*, 302–3; emphasis in the original.

Chapter 8

KOLLONTAI ON CLASS, GENDER, AND PATRIARCHY

This chapter examines the contributions of Alexandra Kollontai (1872–1952) to the study of gender, patriarchy, and the position of women in capitalist society and provides an analysis of her views on "the women's question," as well as the processes engendering the social emancipation of women.[1]

Kollontai was one of the most outspoken proponents of women's rights at the beginning of this century. Keenly aware of the oppression of women in capitalist society and adamantly opposed to the patriarchal structures imposed on women that assured their subordination over the centuries, Kollontai took up the study of the women's question to advance the cause of women's rights and thereby contribute to women's total social emancipation. To this end, she undertook a serious study of the nature and dynamics of women's oppression in contemporary capitalist society and thus helped develop a theory and practice for the liberation of women.

Capitalism, Patriarchy, and the Women's Question

The principal idea in the approach taken by Kollontai to the women's question, which sharply differed from that adopted by her feminist contemporaries, was the recognition of existing social relations—above all, relations of production or class relations—as the determinant of various aspects of life in class society, including the subordination and oppression of women. "The conditions and forms of production," Kollontai wrote in *The Social Basis of the Women's Question*, "have subjugated women throughout human history, and have gradually relegated them to the position of oppression and dependence in which most of them existed until now."[2] Pointing out that "specific economic factors were behind the subordination of women"[3] throughout history, she went on to argue that:

> A colossal upheaval of the entire social and economic structure was required before women could begin to retrieve the significance

> and independence they had lost. . . . The same forces which for thousands of years enslaved women now, at a further stage of development, are leading them along the path of freedom and independence.[4]

This is so because class society in general, and capitalism in particular, is producing and reproducing its class contradictions. By drawing in more and more women into the labor force and exploiting them at a level much higher than working men, Kollontai argued, capitalism is inevitably contributing to the future liberation of women as women begin to organize and struggle alongside men for the liberation of their class, working class—an observation similar to the one made earlier by Engels.

Kollontai's analysis of the nature and sources of women's oppression led her to look for a class solution to the emancipation of women. The rights of women, she argued, could not be achieved while society was organized on the basis of private profit. Going beyond the critique of capitalism and the exploitation of labor in general, Kollontai placed the interests of women workers at the forefront of her analysis and examined the struggles of working women and their families in the late-nineteenth-century capitalist society that preceded the bourgeois women's movement that emerged later during this period, bringing into sharp focus the class content of women's rights under capitalism.

Examining the origins of the bourgeois women's movement, Kollontai traced the development of a broader struggle for women's rights as it unfolded during the second half of the nineteenth century. Viewing the condition of women from a class perspective, Kollontai differentiated the interests of working-class women from those of bourgeois and petty bourgeois women and argued that well before the birth of the bourgeois women's movement, working class women had entered the world of labor and struggled for their rights as part of the struggles of the working class in general. This class-based approach to the women's question allowed her to reach different political conclusions than the bourgeois feminists of her time and laid bare the ideological split that defined the two leading positions in the early women's movement.

Class, Gender, and Feminism

Providing a class-analysis approach to the study of women's position in capitalist society, Kollontai, like Rosa Luxemburg and Clara Zetkin, defined the rights and interests of women on the basis of their *class* position, not their gender alone. She developed a sharp critique of the feminist movement for representing the interests of only a segment of the female population—bourgeois women. Siding with the working class politically and advocating the transformation of capitalist society and the building of socialism, Kollontai focused her attention on *working women* and saw their emancipation as part of the process of emancipation of the working class from capitalist exploitation.

Stating her position in sharp contrast to that of the feminists, Kollontai framed the women's question in strictly *class* terms. "The women's world," she wrote, "is divided, just as is the world of men, into two camps":

> The interests and aspirations of one group of women bring it close to the bourgeois class, while the other group has close connections with the proletariat, and its claims for liberation encompass a full solution to the woman question.[5]

She went on to point out that, although both of these groups advocate the liberation of women from their historic oppression, their goals and interests are different because "each of the groups unconsciously takes its starting point from the interests of its own class."[6]

The class essence of women's rights, as manifested in the position of women in society with respect to labor, is clearly driven home in Kollontai's works when she focuses on the problems of working women as they experience them in their daily lives. The abstract, generalized pronouncements of feminist organizations, advocating women's rights in a broader context of female oppression in capitalist society, are thus given concrete meaning in Kollontai's works as she addresses the manifestations of production based on private profit. The exploitation of labor, especially female labor, takes on a special *class* meaning, differentiating the experiences and thereby the interests of women of different classes—a distinction that has important political implications as well. This is pointed out very clearly in much of Kollontai's writings that directly address the feminists.

"The feminists," she points out, "seek equality in the framework of the existing class society; in no way do they attack the basis of this society. They fight for prerogatives for themselves, without challenging the existing prerogatives and privileges."[7] Thus, "however apparently radical the demands of the feminists," she argues, "one must not lose sight of the fact that the feminists cannot, on account of their class position, fight for that fundamental transformation of the contemporary economic and social structure of society without which the liberation of women cannot be complete."[8]

The liberation of working women, and of women in general, cannot therefore be achieved without a major transformation of the existing capitalist social order, which requires, for Kollontai, a revolutionary restructuring of the social, economic, and political life that defined the cultural parameters of society in the early twentieth century.

Social Revolution and the Liberation of Women

The fundamental question for Kollontai regarding the liberation of women was the nature and source of change, which divided the women's movement along class lines. Should women's struggles primarily focus on the manifestations of existing exploitative relations in capitalist society, or should they confront head-on the very structures of capitalism that have generated these manifestations in the first place? Kollontai puts the question this way: "Can political equality in the context of the retention of the entire capitalist-exploiter system free the working woman from that abyss of evil and suffering which pursues and oppresses her both as a woman and as a human being?"[9] And she answers it as follows:

> The more aware among proletarian women realize that neither political nor juridical equality can solve the women's question in all its aspects. While women are compelled to sell their labor power and bear the yoke of capitalism, while the present exploitative system of producing new values continues to exist, they cannot become free and independent persons.[10]

Thus, the aim of the women workers, Kollontai points out, "is to abolish all privileges deriving from birth or wealth" and that in this sense they are "fighting for the common class cause, while at the same time outlining and putting forward those needs and demands that most nearly affect themselves as women, housewives and mothers."[11] The struggles of working women, therefore, "are part and parcel of the common workers' cause!"[12]

> There was a time when working men thought that they alone must bear on their shoulders the brunt of the struggle against capital, that they alone must deal with the "old world" without the help of their womenfolk. However, as working-class women entered the labor market by need, by the fact that husband or father is unemployed, working men became aware that to leave women behind in the ranks of the "non-class-conscious" was to damage their cause and hold it back. The greater the number of conscious fighters, the greater the chances of success. . . .
>
> Every special, distinct form of work among the women of the working class is simply a means of arousing the consciousness of the woman worker and drawing her into the ranks of those fighting for a better future. . . . [The] meticulous work undertaken to arouse the self-consciousness of the woman worker are serving the cause . . . of the unification of the working class.[13]

It is in this context of the broader interests of the working class as a whole that Kollontai developed her understanding of the interplay between class, gender, and patriarchy and identified the centrality of the exploitation of labor for private profit as the basis of the oppression and exploitation of working women in capitalist society.

Notes

1. For a brief biographical sketch of Kollontai, see the excellent compilation on numerous women social theorists by Mary Jo Deegan, ed., *Women in Sociology* (Westport, Conn.: Greenwood Press, 1991), 231–38. See also Sheila Rowbotham, *Women, Resistance, and Revolution* (New York: Penguin, 1972), 134–60.

2. Alexandra Kollontai, "The Social Basis of the Woman Question," in *Selected Writings of Alexandra Kollontai*, ed. Alix Holt (Westport, Conn.: Lawrence Hill, 1978), 61.

3. Ibid., 58.

4. Ibid., 61.

5. Ibid., 59.

6. Ibid.

7. Ibid.

8. Ibid., 59–60.

9. Kollontai, in I.M. Dazhina et al., eds., *Alexandra Kollontai: Selected Articles and Speeches* (New York: International Publishers, 1984), 33–34.

10. Ibid., 34.

11. Ibid., 64.

12. Ibid.

13. Ibid., 62–65.

Chapter 9

DU BOIS AND FRAZIER ON RACE, CLASS, AND SOCIAL EMANCIPATION

This chapter examines the ideas of two of the most prominent black social theorists of the early twentieth century, William Edward Burghardt Du Bois (1868–1963) and Edward Franklin Frazier (1894–1962).[1] Together, Du Bois and Frazier set the standard for the study of race relations in the United States in the early decades of this century and made a major contribution to social theory on the relationship between race and class.

Race Relations and the Color Line

At the beginning of the twentieth century, in 1901, W.E.B. Du Bois proclaimed: "The problem of the twentieth century is the problem of the color line."[2] Subsequently, Frazier, following his mentor, undertook the study of race relations in America to expose the predicament of African Americans, documenting the nature and depth of their oppression. Despite their political differences, together Du Bois and Frazier made a major contribution to the sociology of race and race relations in America in the twentieth century.

W.E.B. Du Bois, writes Meyer Weinberg, "was one of the greatest intellectuals America ever produced. If the intellectual is a tensor between scholarship and social action, Du Bois fulfilled the role with the highest distinction."[3] In his "Foreword" to Manning Marable's biography of Du Bois, John Milton Cooper, Jr., writes:

> W.E.B. Du Bois ranks, along with Frederick Douglass, Booker T. Washington, and Martin Luther King, Jr., as one of the four greatest black Americans in the nation's history. Like them, he was a leader of his people and a man who sought to share fully in their lot. . . . [M]ore than any other person, he uncovered and interpreted black Americans' African roots and theorized about their ties to the larger nonwhite world. Du Bois deserves the title of first and greatest Afro-American.[4]

"There is no outstanding Afro-American creative figure of the twentieth century," writes another distinguished historian and editor of Du Bois's numerous works, Herbert Aptheker, "who did not, at some point, draw inspiration and gather aid directly from their Dean."[5] Indeed, Du Bois was the most celebrated intellectual and social activist in the black community until his death in 1963.

E. Franklin Frazier was among those exposed to Du Bois's ideas while a graduate student at Howard University—ideas that shaped the content and direction of studies taken up by a new generation of black intellectuals in subsequent decades. "Frazier's work and self-identity," writes Anthony Platt, "were consistently driven by a sense of moral outrage at any kind of social inequality and a relentless, burning hatred of racism."[6]

> Although his contributions were much more modest, Frazier was no less political than Du Bois. They made different kinds of contributions and operated in different arenas, but, like Du Bois, it was a rare day when Frazier did not think about the struggle against inequality.[7]

Concerned at the same time with the social makeup of the black community and its internal class dynamics, which were in the process of maturation, Frazier addressed the developing class distinctions that were increasingly determining the nature and dynamics of social relations among blacks in the mid twentieth century—trends that developed further in the latter part of the century.[8]

Placed in historical context, the ideas and works of Du Bois and Frazier provide us much insight into the social condition of African Americans over the past two hundred years and give us the tools of analysis to develop an interpretation of their predicament in American society.

From Slavery to Freedom: The Predicament of African Americans

Under slavery and formal freedom, the African American experience is captured brilliantly in the works of W.E.B. Du Bois, whose great-grandfather was a slave. Born barely two years after the end of the Civil War, Du Bois became keenly aware of the experience of slavery in the social, economic, political, and psychological makeup of African Americans in the closing decades of the nineteenth century.

The slave system in the South set the parameters of life for millions of black slaves who were denied citizenship and basic human rights for more than a century.

> With the new world came fatally the African slave trade and Negro slavery in the Americas. There were new cruelties, new hatreds of

> human beings, and new degradations of human labor. The temptation to degrade human labor was made vaster and deeper by the incredible accumulation of wealth based on slave labor, by the boundless growth of greed, and by world-wide organization for new agricultural crops, new techniques in industry, and world-wide trade.[9]

The slaves, Du Bois explains, "could be bought and sold, could move from place to place only with permission, were forbidden to learn to read or write, legally could never hold property or marry."[10] This oppressive condition that the slaves experienced continued until the late nineteenth century.

> Then came the war, which was not started with the idea of liberating the slaves, but which soon showed the North that freedom for the Negro was not only a logical conclusion of the war, but the only possible physical conclusion. Two hundred thousand black men were drafted in the army and the whole slave support to the Confederacy was threatened with withdrawal. Insurrection was in the air and the emancipation of the slaves was needed to save the Union. . . .
>
> The Negro was freed as a penniless, landless, naked, ignorant laborer. Very few Negroes owned property in the South; a larger number of the race in the South were field hands, servants of the lowest class.[11]

Over the years, the ex-slaves became transformed into farm laborers and then into industrial workers in the mines and mills of modern capital as wage labor. Thus, during the century following emancipation, more and more blacks became part of an expanding working class, and the black community in general began to undergo internal social differentiation such that a more complex class structure began to emerge among blacks as well. The intersection of race and class thus took on new meaning in the discussions and debates that began to surface among black intellectuals in addressing the problems of race and class in contemporary American society.

The Question of Race and Class

The changing dynamics of the developing class structure among blacks led Du Bois and Frazier to take up a closer examination of the relationship between race and class.

Du Bois had earlier (at the turn of the century) observed that "the problem of the twentieth century is the problem of the color line," and by the early 1920s had rejected the class analysis approach to the study of black people in America by asking: "How far, for instance, does the dogma of the 'class struggle' apply to black folk in the United States today?"[12] He answered it this way:

> The colored group is not yet divided into capitalists and laborers. There are only the beginnings of such a division. In one hundred years, if we develop along conventional lines, we would have such fully separated classes.[13]

Although he continued to hold on to these views during the 1930s and 1940s, Du Bois was always aware of the potential development of classes and class conflict among blacks if current trends of capitalist expansion in America were to encroach on the black community in the future:

> The main danger and the central question of the capitalistic development through which the Negro-American group is forced to go is the question of the ultimate control of the capital which they must raise and use. If this capital is going to be controlled by a few men for their own benefit, then we are destined to suffer from our own capitalists exactly what we are suffering from white capitalists today.[14]

By midcentury, the dynamics of the changing class structure among blacks that was manifesting itself in the black community convinced Du Bois to supplement his earlier observations by stating:

> [During the 1930s] I repudiated the idea that Negroes were in danger of inner class division based on income and exploitation. Here again I was wrong. Twenty years later, by 1950, it was clear that the great machine of big business was sweeping not only the mass of white Americans . . . it had also and quite naturally swept Negroes into the same maelstrom.[15]

He went on to point out that, with the fall of official segregation in public accommodations and schools, blacks "will be divided into classes even more sharply than now."[16] By 1960, Manning Marable points out, "Du Bois argued that 'class divisions' within Negro communities had so divided blacks 'that they are no longer [one] single body. They are different sets of people with different sets of interests.'"[17]

Adopting more and more a class-analysis approach to the race question, Du Bois during the later years of his life (in the 1950s and early 1960s), as Gerald Horne points out, began to develop "firm and decided views about the basis for race discrimination" in class terms: "He continually pointed to the wage differential between black and white workers as the material basis for racism."[18] In this way, Horne observes, "Du Bois was edging away" from his earlier view that "the problem of the twentieth century is the problem of the color line" and "edging toward the view that the twentieth century's problem was labor."[19]

Frazier, like Du Bois, also went through a transformation in his ideas on the causes and consequences of racism. Going beyond his earlier, social-psychological studies of race relations and the black family, Frazier's views about racism later became more and more informed by social class.[20] "Influenced by the class-based theories of left intellectuals and organizations," writes Platt, "by the 1930s . . . his writings tended to reinterpret the history of race relations through a prism of exploitation."[21]

"The introduction of the Negro into America," Frazier pointed out, "was due to the economic expansion of Europe" and "the fate of Negro slavery was determined by economic forces"; in this sense, "the Negro's status in the United States," he stressed, "has been bound up, in the final analysis, with the role which the Negro has played in the economic system."[22] Framing the problem in such broader, historical and structural terms, Frazier, as Platt points out, "located the fundamental roots of racism in the dynamics of class relations on a global scale."[23]

Racism, Class Conflict, and Social Emancipation

Both Du Bois and Frazier understood the dynamics of racism as a manifestation of class conflict. They understood, therefore, that social emancipation would be the outcome of a resolution of the struggle between the chief opposing classes in society. Although Du Bois's views on the forms the struggle would take differed from Frazier's, both agreed on the necessity of social change to end exploitation and bring about peaceful relations between the races.

Whereas Du Bois argued in favor of gradual transformation of social relations through reforms, Frazier opted for a more concrete assessment of the historical record and saw no other viable alternative to resolve the race question except through a radical transformation of the existing social-economic order. Thus Du Bois expected, earlier in the century, "changes to come mainly through reason, human sympathy, and the education of children" and "gravely doubt[ed] if, in the future, there will be any real recurrent necessity for upheaval."[24] However, the absence of any progress in race relations in subsequent decades led to his skepticism on the viability of this approach in the later years of his life, which, given his rejection of a revolutionary alternative to rejuvenate the movement, led him to political resignation and defeatism.

Frazier's stance was much more forceful and direct, allowing no pessimism of will or resolve. In contrast to Du Bois's reformist approach, Frazier argued that there could be "no fundamental changes in race relations . . . unless these changes are brought about in connection with some revolutionary movement."[25] However well intentioned, "the accumulation of goodwill will not do it," he added, because "the present racial situation is bound up with the present economic and social system."[26]

Advancing a reformist stance in line with the position of the National Association for the Advancement of Colored People (NAACP), with which he was associated for nearly twenty-five years,[27] Du Bois opted for limited political action within the established juridical boundaries of the system, instead of challenging it at its foundations. Although he expressed his skepticism with regard to the franchise as a way out of racial oppression, he advocated dissent through existing political channels, but remained indifferent to mass mobilization from below—a mobilization that was later successfully developed by more active leaders in the civil rights movement, such as Martin Luther King, Jr.

Frazier's views, however, were characteristically more radical and more militant, which pitted him and other activists against what he considered elitist intellectuals who stood apart from the masses and failed to take the necessary political steps to facilitate their liberation. This political divide helped fuel Frazier's views on the black upper and middle classes whom he despised as self-centered clones of their white counterparts, driven solely by their class interests.

While the changing class composition of the black community, which further intensified in the 1970s, gave rise to the subsequent debate on the caste and class controversy between William Julius Wilson, Charles Willie, and others in a different context,[28] Frazier's anticipation of the development of a new dynamic through the evolving contradictions of capitalist development in the late twentieth century led him to optimistic conclusions on the possibility of black-white unity within the working class, targeting the capitalists as the source of racial oppression and class exploitation—exploitation of an increasingly multiracial, multinational working class. Drawing his optimism on this score from the effects of the Great Depression on the working class in the 1930s and observing the "spread of radical ideas among working class Negroes through cooperation with white workers",[29] Frazier projected that "as the Negro may become an integral part of the proletariat, . . . the feeling against his color may break down in the face of a common foe."[30] Clarifying his position on the interplay of race, class, and social emancipation, "in the urban environment," he wrote, the black worker "is showing signs of understanding the struggle for power between the proletariat and the owning classes, and is beginning to cooperate with white workers in this struggle which offers the only hope of his complete emancipation."[31]

Despite their differences in political approach to the strategy and tactics of the struggle against racism and racial oppression, Du Bois and Frazier were two of the most prominent black intellectuals and social activists of the twentieth century; in their own distinct ways, they gave their utmost to this struggle and worked toward the building of a society based on equality among all citizens, regardless of race, gender, or class. In this sense, these two champions of human rights were among the pioneers of the modern civil rights movement that emerged toward the end of their lives. Yet, some three decades after their death, and nearly a century after the pronouncements of Du Bois on "the problem of the color line," racism and racial oppression continue to afflict American society. And in response to it, the fight against racism and for social justice continues to grow and intensify in these final years of the twentieth century.

Notes

1. See James E. Blackwell and Morris Janowitz, eds., *Black Sociologists: Historical and Contemporary Perspectives* (Chicago: University of Chicago Press, 1974).

2. W.E.B. Du Bois, in *The Atlantic Monthly* 87 (1901), 354.

3. Meyer Weinberg, ed., *W.E.B. Du Bois: A Reader* (New York: Harper & Row, 1970), xv.

4. John Milton Cooper, Jr., "Foreword," in Manning Marable, *W.E.B. Du Bois: Black Radical Democrat* (Boston: Twayne, 1986), vii.

5. Herbert Aptheker, "W.E.B. Du Bois: Struggle Not Despair," *Clinical Sociology Review* 8 (1990): 62–63. For an extensive list of Du Bois's works, see Herbert Aptheker, *Annotated Bibliography of the Published Writings of W.E.B. Du Bois* (Millwood, N.Y.: Kraus-Thomson Organization, 1973).

6. Anthony M. Platt, *E. Franklin Frazier Reconsidered* (New Brunswick, N.J.: Rutgers University Press, 1991), 3.

7. Ibid.

8. For an analysis of these developments, see E. Franklin Frazier, *Black Bourgeoisie* (Glencoe, Ill.: Free Press, 1957).

9. W.E.B. Du Bois, "The White Masters of the World," in *The Writings of W.E.B. Du Bois*, ed. Virginia Hamilton (New York: Crowell, 1975), 201–2.

10. W.E.B. Du Bois, "The Social Effects of Emancipation," in Weinberg, *W.E.B. Du Bois: A Reader*, 71.

11. Ibid., 72.

12. W.E.B. Du Bois, "The Class Struggle," in Weinberg, *W.E.B. Du Bois: A Reader*, 341.

13. Ibid., 341.

14. Ibid., 342–43.

15. Du Bois, quoted in Gerald Home, *Black & Red: W.E.B. Du Bois and the Afro-American Response to the Cold War, 1944–1963* (Albany: SUNY Press, 1986), 224.

16. W.E.B. Du Bois, "Negroes and the Crisis of Capitalism in the United States," *Monthly Review* 4, no. 12 (April 1953): 482–83.

17. Marable, *W.E.B. Du Bois*, 207.

18. Home, *Black & Red*, 225.

19. Ibid., 224.

20. For his earlier studies, see, for example, E. Franklin Frazier, *The Negro Family in the United States* (Chicago: University of Chicago Press, 1939). His later views on the relationship of race and class are developed in E. Franklin Frazier, *The Negro in the United States* (New York: Macmillan, 1949); and idem, *Race and Culture Contacts in the Modern World* (New York: Knopf, 1957).

21. Platt, *E. Franklin Frazier Reconsidered*, 164.

22. Frazier, quoted in ibid., 164.

23. Ibid., 219.

24. Du Bois, "The Class Struggle," in Weinberg, *W.E.B. Du Bois: A Reader*, 341.

25. Frazier, quoted in Platt, *E. Franklin Frazier Reconsidered*, 186.

26. Ibid.

27. Du Bois was one of the principal founders of the NAACP in 1909 and for nearly twenty-five years served as editor of its official publication, *The Crisis*.

28. This controversy, which began with the publication of William Julius Wilson's *The Declining Significance of Race* (Chicago: University of Chicago Press, 1978) and continued through his *The Truly Disadvantaged: The Inner City, the Underclass, and Public Policy* (Chicago: University of Chicago Press, 1987), took place within the context of the changing dynamics of the class structure within the black community resulting from the transformation of the U.S. economy and its impact on urban centers, which gave rise to an "underclass" of largely unemployed or menially employed black people trapped in America's inner cities. For an overview of the different positions taken in this debate, see the chapter on "Wilson and Willie on Race, Class, and Poverty" in Part II of this book.

29. Frazier, quoted in Platt, *E. Franklin Frazier Reconsidered*, 164.

30. Ibid., 163.

31. Ibid., 164.

PART II
CONTEMPORARY SOCIAL THEORY

Chapter 10

PARSONS, MERTON, AND FUNCTIONALIST THEORY

This chapter examines the central ideas presented in the works of Talcott Parsons, Robert K. Merton, and other functionalist theorists who came to dominate American sociology during the 1950s.[1] It critically analyzes their concept of human nature, social organization, and the social system.

Human Nature

In the process of development of a theory of social systems Parsons and other functionalists have made a number of assumptions about human nature. These assumptions constitute an integral part of contemporary functionalist theory. In this sense, the functionalist view of social organization, society, and the social system cannot be understood clearly unless we first comprehend the nature and theoretical underpinnings of these assumptions concerning the place of the individual in the social system.

In the Parsonian scheme, the basic alternatives that in certain combinations orient the individual actor to his or her culture and social system are referred to as the "pattern variables."[2] These are the dichotomies of (1) affectivity vs. affective neutrality, (2) self-orientation vs. collectivity orientation, (3) universalism vs. particularism, (4) achievement vs. ascription, and (5) specificity vs. diffuseness.[3] Parsons believes that the value orientation of the culture in which the individual finds himself or herself can be described in terms of these dichotomies. The individual learns this value orientation through the process of socialization and social control, which together facilitate the internalization of society's values. It is this internalization of value orientation patterns by individuals that keeps society going, according to Parsons.

Merton's approach to norms and values is likewise based on a process wherein an individual's values correspond to roles by way of "role performance."[4] Through this process, the person responds to other individuals only in terms of the defined expectations of acceptable behavior between them. Hence this near-mechanical view of individuals allows for the subsequent development of conformity and equilibrium.

Going beyond the traditional Parsonian frame of functional analysis and introducing into the model "middle range" theories that can be empirically examined, Merton has contributed an additional dimension to contemporary functionalist theory by identifying "manifest" and "latent" functions.[5] Manifest functions are those that are recognized and intended by the participants, whereas latent functions are those that are not recognized and have unintended consequences: "The distinction between manifest and latent functions was devised to preclude the inadvertent confusion, often found in the sociological literature, between conscious *motivations* for social behavior and its *objective consequences*."[6]

Thus while poverty in capitalist society is a deplorable condition of life for some (unemployed and poorly paid) segments of the population who find themselves in such a condition, it also serves as a latent function to justify the necessity for hard work so that employed workers continue to generate profits for their employers, with the threat that failing to do so would force them into unemployment and poverty. Hence, as in this case, latent functions are often the result of actions designed to benefit powerful social forces in society—forces that have an interest in securing conformity to the dominant values, ideas, and norms in society.

The individual, according to Parsons, Merton, and other functionalists, is built on the notion of conformity. Conformity of individuals is seen as crucial for the maintenance of the system. To illustrate this point clearly, Parsons explicitly states that

> the concept "integration" . . . is a mode of relation of the units of a system by virtue of which, on the one hand, they act so as collectively to avoid disrupting the system and making it impossible to maintain its stability, and, on the other hand, to "co-operate" to promote its functioning as a unity.[7]

Thus, "the well-integrated personality," writes Parsons,

> feels an obligation to live up to expectations in his variously defined roles, to be a "good boy" to be a "good student," an "efficient worker," and so on. . . . The element of obligation in this sense is properly treated as "disinterested." It is a matter of "identification" with a generalized pattern, conformity with which is "right."[8]

According to the functionalist view, then, is that individuals acquire a sense of satisfaction when their behavior fulfills the expectations of the social group or society to which they belong and which sets the standards for individual behavior in varied social settings. As a result, the fulfillment of these goals becomes a motivational objective of individuals so that the resultant behavior is oriented toward the attainment of these goals. In this way, society achieves the integration of individuals into the social system and thereby secures social order and stability in the system. The crucial part in Parsons's system, then, is the internalization of value patterns by individuals in order to assure the maintenance of the social system. This internalization, Parsons argues, "constitutes the strategic element of [the] basic personality structure" because it is only in this way that social order can be obtained.[9]

Merton's equally central concern with conformity and integration leads him to observe that deviation from the norms established in society is a result of role or status strain or is a response to the divergence between socially established common goals and differentially distributed means. Acknowledging the prevalence and impact of such strains on society, Merton introduces into his model elements that are "dysfunctional" to the system.[10] Deviance is one such element that represents a dysfunctional relationship of the individual to society. If the deviance exceeds the acceptable range of tolerance and if the deviant cannot be persuaded to adopt an alternate role, the resultant variance and diversity within the social system creates the need for social control.[11] Thus, with the imposition of social control to maintain both the value patterns of a society as well as the motivation of its members, Parsons and Merton bring us full swing into their stable, functional social system.

Society and the Social System

The modern functionalists see society as a system of interdependent parts that are integrated through institutionalized norms and patterns of behavior.[12] Such integration, argues Parsons, assures the maintenance of the social system:

> Solidarity is the generalized capacity of agencies in the society to "bring into line" the behavior of system units in accordance with the integrative needs of the system, to check or reverse disruptive tendencies to deviant behavior, and to promote the conditions of harmonious cooperation.[13]

Thus the functionalist view of society is concerned with the relationship of equilibrating forces between the various parts of the system. As each part or unit of the system is given equal importance, any change in one part will affect all the others. To maintain conditions of stability within the system, society must be in a state of "equilibrium"—one that promotes the survival and maintenance of the prevailing social system. Such rationalization, however, has led critics to charge that modern functionalist theory legitimizes mid-twentieth-century dominant capitalist ideology. Indeed, this is clearly evident in their discussion of social classes, politics, and the state.

Generally, the functionalists see social classes and class inequality as naturally occurring phenomena in all societies at all times. In their classic essay, "Some Principles of Stratification," Kingsley Davis and Wilbert Moore speak of "the *universal necessity* which calls forth stratification in any social system."[14] Moreover, "the main functional necessity explaining the universal presence of stratification," write Davis and Moore, "is precisely the *requirement* faced by any society of placing and motivating individuals in the social structure."[15]

> Inevitably, then, a society must have, first, some kind of rewards that it can use as inducements, and second, some way of distributing these rewards differentially according to positions. The rewards and their distribution become a part of the social order, and thus give rise to stratification.[16]

This is so, Davis and Moore categorically state, in "every society, no matter how simple or complex."[17]

Such an assertion, however, is based on the functionalist (ideological) assumption that stratification is "functionally necessary" to ensure *the maintenance of the existing social system* and not a scientific analysis of historical reality. "Functional theories," comments Arthur Stinchcombe, "are like other scientific theories: they have empirical consequences which are either true or false. Deciding whether they are true or false is not a theoretical or ideological matter but an empirical one."[18] As wealth of data available on a large number of primitive societies show, almost all (98 percent) of hunting and gathering (primitive communal) societies do *not* have a class system or structured social inequality, while the remaining 2 percent have become "stratified" as a result of contact with more advanced societies.[19] Hence, as humans have lived in primitive hunting and gathering societies as the predominant form of social organization for most of human history, it is clear that the historical evolution of homosapiens for thousands of years has been unquestionably highly democratic and egalitarian. Only in more recent times do we begin to see the development of class systems, hence of class inequality.[20]

To his credit, Melvin M. Tumin, a functionalist himself, has expressed strong criticism of the Davis-Moore thesis, refuting the latter's contentions on inequality and stratification. In fact, Tumin's critical analysis of the problem leads him to reach almost exactly the opposite conclusions from those of Davis and Moore, as he specifies various "negative functions, or dysfunctions, of institutionalized social inequality," such as "human ignorance, war, poverty."[21] Responding to the Davis-Moore thesis on the functional necessity of inequality, Tumin raises some important issues that challenge this view. He writes:

> Since a theoretical model can be devised in which all other clearly indispensable major social functions are performed, but in which inequality as motive and reward is absent, how then account for stratification in terms of structural and functional necessities and inevitabilities?[22]

Extending his analysis to account for the key mechanism that perpetuates structured social inequality, "an essential characteristic of all known kinship systems," writes Tumin,

> is that they function as transmitters of inequalities from generation to generation. Similarly, an essential characteristic of all known stratification systems is that they employ the kinship system as their agent of transmission of inequalities.
>
> To the extent that this is true, then it is true by definition that the elimination from kinship systems of their function as transmitters of inequalities (and hence the alteration of the definition of kinship systems) would eliminate those inequalities which were generation-linked.
>
> Obviously, the denial to parents of their ability and right to transmit both advantages and disadvantages to their offspring would require a fundamental alteration in all existing concepts of kinship structure. At the least, there would have to be a vigilant separation maintained between the unit which reproduces and the unit which socializes, maintains and places. In theory, this separation is eminently possible. In practice, it would be revolutionary.[23]

Indeed it would! By curbing the transfer of wealth and property through the alteration of the nature and function of the kinship structure, it is indeed possible to bring up a new generation of individuals without the necessity of a significant level of social inequality.

Power, Politics, and the State

Turning to politics, Parsons and other contemporary functionalists have characterized the modern U.S. state as a democratic institution whose primary function is to secure order within the system.[24] Representing the interests of society as a whole, the state coordinates the other major institutions of society—economic, educational, religious, and so on—and advances both the general social welfare and that of the individuals within it. Thus, for the functionalists, while the state provides strong, effective leadership and represents institutionalized power and authority vis-à-vis individual citizens, its actions reflect widespread and diverse interests that exist in society—interests that the functionalists claim are well represented within the state. As the supreme guardian of "representative democracy," the state thus fulfills its role in carrying out its social tasks while ensuring its democratic control by society.

"Power," writes Parsons, "is a generalized facility or resource in the society":

> It has to be divided or allocated, but it also has to be produced and it has collective as well as distributive functions. It has the capacity to mobilize the resources of the society for the attainment of goals for which a general "public" commitment has been made, or may be made. It is mobilization, above all, of the action of persons and groups, which is *binding* on them by virtue of their position in the society.[25]

Thus the state maintains an autonomous role for itself as the sole public authority and at the same time assures the equal distribution of power across competing political groups in society. "This tension in functionalist thinking on the state between a view of the necessity for a strong, modernizing, central co-ordinator on the one hand, and a relatively equal distribution of social powers on the other," observes one critic, "reflects the cross-pulls from two allegedly functional pre-requisites: the need for autonomy and the need for integration."[26] By distributing its control among a broad range of social groups and preventing its monopolization by any one group, the state, according to the functionalists, thus paves the way for political competition and "pluralist democracy."[27]

Empirical reality, however, is much different from what contemporary functionalists would have us believe. While functionalists such as Robin Williams argue that "no 'rule by monopoly' is in sight in the American economy" and "corporate shares are held by large numbers of individuals," and further, that the American pattern of power distribution is "the balancing of interests and compromising of conflicts through multiple power-centers, numerous separate channels of influence, and the subdivision of political authorities,"[28] the true extent of wealth/ownership and of political power can be illustrated as follows: the top 10 percent of American families own 78 percent of real estate, 90 percent of all publicly held corporate stocks, 90 percent of all bonds, and 94 percent of net business assets.[29] Moreover, the top one-half of

1 percent of all families own nearly half of all corporate stocks and bonds, and nearly two-thirds of all business assets.[30] Further, the two hundred largest U.S. corporations, many of which are mutually controlled through interlocking directorates, control more than 75 percent of all corporately held assets and account for nearly two-thirds of total net profits.[31]

Conclusion

The functionalist conception of human nature, society, and politics examined in this chapter reveals that contemporary functionalists have uncritically accepted existing structures and conditions of capitalist society as givens and have thus contributed, implicitly or explicitly, toward the maintenance of the existing social order and the perpetuation of dominant capitalist ideology. This has opened the way to a barrage of criticism of modern functionalism for being nothing more than an ideological expression of the capitalist system in the United States.

The functionalist contention that in America political power resides with many diverse and equally powerful groups reflecting the interests of the vast majority of the population has similarly come under strong criticism in recent decades. In the late 1950s, critics, led by C. Wright Mills, began to provide a powerful critique of Parsonian functionalism that set the stage for subsequent debates within sociology. Expanding this effort during the 1960s and 1970s, G. William Domhoff and numerous other critical sociologists were instrumental in widening the critique of modern functionalism and thus breaking its decades-long monopoly over social theory.

It is through such critique of the ideological implications of modern functionalist theory vis-à-vis its earlier intellectual hegemony within sociology that more and more sociologists have come to understand clearly the dynamics of recent developments in contemporary sociological theory. The contributions to this critique through alternative theoretical formulations provided by Mills and Domhoff are discussed in subsequent chapters of this book.

Notes

1. Although this chapter addresses two different versions of contemporary functionalist theory—Parsonian and Mertonian, or what C. Wright Mills called "Grand Theory" and "Abstracted Empiricism," respectively—we use the term "functionalism" when referring to both versions.

2. Talcott Parsons, *The Social System* (New York: Free Press, 1951), 67.

3. Ibid.

4. Robert K. Merton, *Social Theory and Social Structure* (New York: Free Press, 1968), 390–94.

5. Ibid., 114–18.

6. Ibid., 114.

7. Parsons, *Essays in Sociological Theory*, rev. ed. (Glencoe, Ill.: Free Press, 1954), 71.

8. Ibid., 56–57.

9. Parsons, *The Social System*, 228.

10. Merton, *Social Theory and Social Structure*, 105.

11. Ibid., 230–48.

12. Harry M. Johnson, *Sociology: A Systematic Introduction* (New York: Harcourt, Brace, 1960).

13. Talcott Parsons, cited in Chandler Morse, "The Functional Imperatives," in *The Social Theories of Talcott Parsons*, ed. Max Black (Englewood Cliffs, N.J.: Prentice Hall, 1961), 126.

14. Kingsley Davis and Wilbert E. Moore, "Some Principles of Stratification," *American Sociological Review* 10, no. 2 (April 1945): 242.

15. Ibid.

16. Ibid., 243.

17. Ibid.

18. Arthur L. Stinchcombe, "Some Empirical Consequences of the Davis-Moore Theory of Stratification," *American Sociological Review* 28 (October 1963): 808.

19. Gerhard Lenski, *Power and Privilege* (New York: McGraw-Hill, 1966); Eleanor B. Leacock, "Introduction," in F. Engels, *The Origin of the Family, Private Property, and the State* (New York: International Publishers, 1972).

20. See Albert Szymanski, *Class Structure* (New York: Praeger, 1983), chap. 2.

21. Melvin Tumin, "Some Principles of Stratification: A Critical Analysis," *American Sociological Review* 18, no. 4 (August 1953): 394; and idem, "Reply to Kingsley Davis," *American Sociological Review* 18, no. 6 (December 1953): 672.

22. Tumin, "Reply to Kingsley Davis," 672.

23. Ibid.

24. Talcott Parsons, *Societies: An Evolutionary Approach* (Englewood Cliffs, N.J.: Prentice Hall, 1966); and idem, "On the Concept of Political Power," in T. Parsons, *Sociological Theory and Modern Society* (New York: Free Press, 1967).

25. Talcott Parsons, *Structure and Process in Modern Societies* (New York: Free Press, 1960), 221.

26. Roger King, *The State in Modern Society* (Chatham, N.J.: Chatham House, 1986), 15.

27. S.N. Eisenstadt, ed., *Modernization: Protest and Change* (Englewood Cliffs, N.J.: Prentice Hall, 1966) cited in King, *The State in Modern Society*, 15.

28. Ibid.

29. Jerry Kloby, "Increasing Class Polarization in the United States: The Growth of Wealth and Income Inequality," in *Critical Perspectives in Sociology*, ed. Berch Berberoglu (Dubuque, Iowa: Kendall/Hunt, 1991), 44.

30. Ibid.

31. U.S. Bureau of the Census, *Statistical Abstract of the United States, 1990* (Washington, D.C.: Government Printing Office, 1990), 541.

Chapter 11

HOMANS ON SOCIAL EXCHANGE*

Social exchange theory is a perspective with a long history in social science circles, extending from Adam Smith and Jeremy Bentham through Peter Blau, Richard Emerson, Mancur Olson, James Coleman, John Thibaut and Harold Kelley to such contemporary practitioners as Karen Cook, Michael Hechter, David Willer, Linda Mohn, John Roemer and John Elster. In this chapter, we focus on George Caspar Homans as exchange theory's trailblazer among American sociologists. Homans not only presented the theory in its clearest and most forceful form; he became the intellectual lightning rod for the adverse reaction it engendered. Homans was the exchange theorist's theorist, and his writings on exchange constitute one of the best known reactions against collectivist explanations of human behavior.

A Move Toward Exchange

Marriage, Authority and Final Causes, a 65-page pamphlet published in 1955, marked Homans' move away from his previous sociological orientation and in the direction of exchange theory.[1] This approach took more definite form in a 1958 article in which he viewed *all human interaction* in terms of *exchange*, a type of bargaining:

> Interaction between persons is an exchange of goods, material and non-material. This is one of the oldest theories of social behavior, and one that we still use everyday to interpret our own behavior, as when we say, "I found so-and-so rewarding"; or "I got a good deal out of him"; or, even, "Talking with him took a good deal out of me."[2]

In this article, Homans spoke of costs, profits, rewards, influence, and distributive justice—all concepts developed in his later writings on exchange. In fact, most of his subsequent work mirrors the topics found here in embryonic form.

*This chapter was written by Larry T. Reynolds and Alice L. Littlefield.

Homans' "all the world's a market" analogizing is, in part, a reaction against Talcott Parsons and his followers and their attempts to impose functionalism on sociology. As Homans sees it, the functionalists have it backwards; we should not be studying society first and individuals last. Rather, we must first examine simple social behavior because "what happens when two or three persons are in a position to influence one another [is] the sort of thing of which those massive structures called 'classes,' 'firms,' 'communities,' and 'societies' must ultimately be composed."[3]

Market Meets Maze: Economics and Behavior

The ideas contained in the 1958 article were considerably expanded in 1961 with the publication of the book *Social Behavior: Its Elementary Forms*.[4] It laid out a sociological theory quite compatible with the folk wisdom of American society. Here Homans assumed, as do most citizens of the United States, that people are materialistic, profit-motivated, and self-interested; that competition is a lever of progress; that market exchange is good exchange; and that capitalism is not only the best but the most natural form of economic organization.

Many sociologists admired this book, and many others took it to task. In response to his critics, Homans offered a revised edition in 1974, in which he argued once again that the best way to conceptualize human interaction is to treat it as exchange. In order to do so, Homans introduced eleven concepts from which he generated the theory's six key postulates. Four of the concepts were taken from classical economics; the remaining seven derive from the behaviorism of the psychologist B. F. Skinner.

The Concepts

The eleven concepts that constitute the core of Homans' theory of social exchange are as follows:

Activity: Behavior attempting to elicit a reward.

Cost: An activity that is punishing, or an alternative reward that is foregone in order to get still another reward.

Distributive justice: Activities involving the calculation of whether costs and investments have led to a "fair" profit by individuals in an exchange.

Interaction: Behaviors in which people direct their activities in order to derive rewards and avoid punishments from each other.

Investments: A person's relevant past activities (such as skills, education, and expertise) and social characteristics (such as sex, age, and race) which are brought to the situation and evaluated by both the person and those with whom one is interacting.

Norms: Verbal statements or activities in which people communicate the kinds of activities that should or should not occur in a situation.

Profit: Rewards, minus the costs and investment, for engaging in a given activity.

Quantity: The number of units of an activity (whether rewarding or punishing) emitted and/or received over a particular period of time.

Rewards: Anything a person receives, or any activity directed toward one that is defined by the person as valuable.

Sentiments: Activities in which individuals communicate their "internal dispositions," such as liking/disliking or approving/disapproving of each other.

Value: An activity's degree of reinforcement or capacity to meet needs of an individual, whether one's own activity or activity directed toward the individual.

Employing these concepts, Homans proceeds to enumerate the key postulates, or basic assumptions, from which nearly everything else in his exchange theory flows.

The Basic Propositions

Homans' perspective on elementary social behavior is anchored in B. F. Skinner's operant conditioning principles, which Homans argued "are the general explanatory propositions of all the social sciences."[5] He saw all large social features as comprised of nothing more than varying combinations of elementary forms of social behavior, the building blocks of complex organizations, social institutions, and social classes. Homans' basic propositions, as modified for the second edition of *Social Behavior: Its Elementary Forms*, are presented below.

(1) The Stimulus Proposition:

"If in the past the occurrence of a particular stimulus, or set of stimuli, has been the occasion on which a person's action has been rewarded, then the more similar the present stimuli are to the past ones, the more likely the person is to perform the action, or some similar action, now."[6]

(2) The Success Proposition:

"For all actions taken by persons, the more often a particular action of a person is rewarded, the more likely the person is to perform that action."[7]

(3) The Value Proposition:

"The more valuable to a person the result of his action, the more likely he is to perform the action."[8]

(4) The Deprivation-Satiation Proposition:

"The more often in the recent past a person has received a particular reward, the less valuable any further unit of that reward becomes for him."[9]

(5) The Aggression-Approval Proposition:

"When a person's action does not receive the reward he expected, or receives punishment he did not expect, he will be angry; he becomes more likely to perform aggressive behavior, and the results of such behavior become more valuable to him. . . . When a person's action received reward as expected, especially a greater reward than he expected, or does not receive punishment he expected, he will be pleased; he will become more likely to perform approving behavior, and the results of such behavior become more valuable to him."[10]

(6) The Rationality Proposition:

"In choosing between alternative actions, a person will choose that one for which, as perceived by him at the time, the value, V, of the result, multiplied by the probability, P, of getting the result, is the greater."[11]

By offering us these propositions, Homans feels he has spelled out the true elementary forms of social behavior and related them to the most fundamental of the social processes, and that larger social features, such as social classes and institutions, flow from them. As Homans sees it, out of basic exchange processes human social organization, at the group and institutional levels, emerges. The emergence follows a pattern, and according to Turner, it is characterized by the following accelerating process:

> 1) Men with capital (reward capacity) "invest" in creating more complex social relations that increase their rewards and allow those whose activities are organized to realize a "profit." 2) With increased rewards, these men can invest in more patterns of organization. 3) Increasingly complex patterns of organization require, first of all, the use of generalized reinforcers, and then, the codification of norms to regulate activity. 4) With this organizational base, it then becomes possible to elaborate further the pattern of organization, creating the necessity for differentiation of subunits that assure the stability of the generalized reinforcers and the integrity of norms. 5) With this differentiation, it is possible to expand even further the networks of interaction, since these are standardized means for rewarding activities and codifying new norms as well as enforcing old rules.[12]

From the vantage point of George C. Homans' exchange theory, large-scale social forms are constructed with the outward expansion of reward capacity, are maintained when they meet individual needs, and begin to crumble when these needs are no longer met.

The six propositions and the eleven concepts detailed above are the corpus of Homans' theory of social exchange. He intends them to explain those features of individual and social life he feels merit attention. But the word "explain" holds a different meaning for him than it does for most of his fellow sociologists. To him, "explain" simply means that if you can show how a given conclusion is a direct deduction from two or more propositions, then you have not only explained the conclusion, but you have said about all you can or need to say about it.[13]

For Homans, a sociological theory is not a series of well-worded, interrelated statements about the sum and substance of social life. It is instead a deductively connected set of laws, and these laws are all psychological in nature; none of them are sociological. Homans successfully relaunched exchange theory along the individualistic route Adam Smith first set for it. Homans' works have met with considerable acclaim, but his variety of exchange theory has some serious shortcomings.

Criticisms

Deutsch has pointed out that Homans' exchange theory is incapable of accounting for novel experience,[14] and Ekeh has argued that Homans' approach offers an intellectual justification for exploitation, suffers from internal inconsistency, and uses inappropriate data for supporting its basic propositions.[15] Abrahamsson attacked Homans on methodological grounds, arguing that he often employed tautological concepts rather than analytical ones.[16] Needham has also argued that Homans used "superficial statistical correlations in place of intensive analysis," and that his exchange theory presents an overly rational image of people. Needham also pointed out that Homans' theory is culturally and temporally limited in its applicability.[17]

Others have emphasized Homans' weak treatment of social organization and social structure,[18] a flaw his theory shares with other forms of social behaviorism, and pointed to the overwhelmingly conservative bias of his approach.

Conclusion

George Caspar Homans' exchange theory has the virtue of being clearly written. It just as clearly requires considerable modification if it is to provide us with an adequate account of larger societal features such as complex organizations, social institutions, social classes, and society itself. Homans' work has served to focus sociologists' thinking on economic matters, but the domination of the contemporary nation-state and of corporate capitalism have led him to believe that social behavior is economic behavior and that human behavior and market behavior are identical—a flaw that stems from a narrow understanding of social structure and social relations that casts doubt on the perspective's ability to explain the diversity of human behavior.

Notes

1. George C. Homans and David Schneider, *Marriage, Authority, and Final Causes* (Glencoe, Ill.: Free Press, 1955).

2. George C. Homans, "Social Behavior as Exchange," *American Journal of Sociology* 63 (1958), 598.

3. Ibid., 597.

4. George C. Homans, *Social Behavior: Its Elementary Forms* (New York: Harcourt, Brace and World, 1961).

5. George C. Homans, *Social Behavior: Its Elementary Forms*, rev. ed. (New York: Harcourt, Brace and Jovanovich, 1974).

6. Ibid., 22–23.

7. Ibid., 16.

8. Ibid., 25.

9. Ibid., 29.

10. Ibid., 37 and 39.

11. Ibid., 43.

12. Jonathan Turner, *The Structure of Sociological Theory* (Homewood, Ill.: Dorsey Press, 1974), 260–61.

13. George C. Homans, "Contemporary Sociological Theory," in Robert E. L. Faris, ed., *Handbook of Modern Sociology* (Chicago: Rand McNallly, 1964), 951.

14. Morton Deutsch, "Homans in the Skinner Box," *Sociological Inquiry* 34 (1964), 156–165.

15. Peter Ekeh, *Social Exchange Theory: The Two Traditions* (Cambridge, Mass.: Harvard University Press, 1974), 127.

16. Bengt Abrahamsson, "Homans on Exchange," *American Journal of Sociology* 76 (1970), 273–285.

17. Rodney Needham, *Structure and Sentiment: A Test Case in Social Anthropology* (Chicago: University of Chicago Press, 1962), 4.

18. Larry T. Reynolds, *Interactionism: Exposition and Critique* (Dix Hills, N.Y.: General Hall, Inc., 1993), 154–157.

Chapter 12

MILLS ON THE POWER ELITE

One of the earliest and most powerful critics of Parsons and structural functionalism in American sociology was C. Wright Mills. Challenging the domain assumptions of the discipline sustained by the functionalist mainstream in the conservative 1950s, Mills soon became one of the most outspoken and controversial social theorists of the postwar period in the United States. Taking on the discipline's domain assumptions singlehandedly, Mills called for the unleashing of "the sociological imagination" to untangle some of the most critical issues of our time—power, politics, and society.[1]

Writing at the height of the Cold War and the McCarthy witch hunts of the 1950s, Mills provided a devastating critique of establishment sociology by launching an all-out attack on Parsonian functionalism, which had played an important role in rationalizing the status quo and thereby promoting the existing social order and reinforcing unequal power relations in society.

This chapter examines the ideas of Mills on the American power structure that he developed as a critique of pluralism. Focusing on his analysis of power relations at the highest levels of American society, the chapter provides a critical overview of his concept of political power, which he presented as an important corrective to the conservative theories of Parsons and what came to be known as Parsonian sociology.

The Power Elite

Influenced by Weber, Mosca, Pareto, and Marx, Mills developed an institutional theory of political power, one based on an articulation of the combined expression of a "power elite." Rejecting the Marxist contention that the capitalist class through its control of the government is also a *ruling* class,[2] Mills adopted an institutional approach, believing that power had shifted from owners of the means of production (or capitalists) to managers and functionaries of the key institutions of American society—the economy, the polity, and, especially, the military.

Such a view forced Mills to focus on high-ranking individual policymakers, especially generals and admirals, whom he considered as part of the higher circles that make up the "power elite":

> Within American society, major national power now resides in the economic, the political, and the military domains. . . . As each of these domains has coincided with the others, as decisions tend to become total in their consequence, *the leading* men in each of the three domains of power—*the warlords, the corporation chieftains, the political directorate*—tend to come together, to form the power elite of America.[3]

The power elite, Mills continues, is composed of those who are "in command of the major hierarchies and organizations of modern society":

> They rule the big corporations. They run the machinery of the state and claim its prerogatives. They direct the military establishment. They occupy the strategic command posts of the social structure.[4]

"The power to make decisions of national and international consequence," Mills points out,

> is now so clearly seated in political, military, and economic institutions that other areas of society seem off to the side. . . . The scattered institutions of religion, education and family are increasingly shaped by the big three, in which history-making decisions now regularly occur. . . . This triangle of power is now a structural fact, and it is the key to any understanding of the higher circles in America today.[5]

The critical point in Mills's analysis of the power elite is not the mere identification of the elite in the three key institutions that constitute the American power structure but the interrelationship between these institutions and between members of the elite that control and direct them:

> The shape and meaning of the power elite today can be understood only when these three sets of structural trends are seen at their point of coincidence. . . . Accordingly, at the top of this structure, the power elite has been shaped by the coincidence of interest between . . . the professional politicians . . . the corporate chieftains and the professional warlords.[6]

The interrelationship between these institutions and between their top leadership is such that retired generals become corporate executives and serve on the boards of directors of large corporations that sell inflated military hardware through lucrative defense contracts signed by old associates in the military, while corporate executives who enter politics serve the interests of big business once they hold key government posts that facilitate the passage of legislation favorable to corporate interests. Thus, as the linkage between big business and the government becomes consolidated, so too the control of the state by business interests becomes solidified, thereby diminishing the prospects for open discussion and debate on public policy:

> The shift of corporation men into the political directorate has accelerated the decline of the politicians in the Congress to the middle levels of power; the formation of the power elite rests in part upon this relegation. It rests also upon the increased official secrecy behind which great decisions are made without benefit of public or even of Congressional debate.[7]

The Rise of the Military

Corresponding to the increased influence over and control of the government by big business, Mills also saw the rise of the military and its more direct role and influence in political affairs, as exemplified by General Dwight D. Eisenhower's ascendance to the presidency in the 1950s. "In so far as the structural clue to the power elite today lies in the enlarged and military state," writes Mills, "that clue becomes evident in the military ascendancy."[8] In a chapter of *The Power Elite* titled "The Military Ascendancy," Mills points out: "As the United States has become a great world power, the military establishment has expanded, and members of its higher echelons have moved directly into diplomatic and political circles."[9] Moreover, "the military order, once a slim establishment in a context of civilian distrust, has become the largest and most expensive feature of government."[10]

> The high military have gained decisive political and economic relevance. The seemingly permanent military threat places a premium upon them and virtually all political and economic actions are now judged in terms of military definitions of reality: the higher military have ascended to a firm position within the power elite of our time.[11]

The ascendancy of the military goes far beyond the institutional boundaries of the political and economic order, according to Mills. The military establishment, he argues, is attempting to extend its power into the civilian sphere by molding public opinion in favor of a military definition of reality:

> It is not only within the higher political and economic, scientific and educational circles that the military ascendancy is apparent. . . .
>
> The military manipulation of civilian opinion and the military invasion of the civilian mind are now important ways in which the power of the warlords is steadily exerted.[12]

The increasing power of the military (and its top leadership) in civilian affairs, Mills contends, "points to the tendency of military men . . . to pursue ends of their own, and to turn other institutional areas into means for accomplishing them."[13] As a result, since World War II, he argues, "those who command the enlarged means of American violence have come to possess considerable autonomy, as well as great influence, among their political and economic colleagues."[14] The generals, he adds, "are now more powerful than they have ever been in the history of the American elite; they have now more means of exercising power in many areas of American life which were previously civilian domains."[15]

Conclusion

The close association of big business, the government, and the military, and between the heads of each of these institutions, led Mills to conclude that, together, this collection of powerful men constitutes the center of power in American society, with the military, through its direct presence in the executive branch, wielding a disproportionate power stemming from the entry of the Pentagon into power politics.

Developments since 1960, however, have shown that the prominence of the military in politics was in effect an outcome of postwar popular sentiment toward a general (Eisenhower) who led the United States to victory in World War II, than the rise of the military, as such, to the center stage of power politics, as Mills's empiricist observations led him to believe. Critics have pointed out that, all appearances to the contrary, his exaggerated emphasis on the rise of the military—hence his (unwarranted) attribution of extraordinary powers to the "warlords," which they contend the latter lacked—has had a lopsided effect on Mills's tripartite model of the power elite.[16] Countering Mills's argument on this point, G. William Domhoff, for example, has pointed out that

> if the United States in the postwar era has adopted what Mills called a military definition of reality, it is because this was chosen

> by leading big business members of the power elite on the basis of their understanding of national goals and international events, not because it was somehow foisted on them by the military.[17]

A more serious criticism of Mills, brought out in subsequent work on the U.S. power structure launched by Domhoff and others in the 1960s, is the absence in Mills's analysis of a connection between the power elite and what Domhoff has called "the social upper class."[18] Herbert Aptheker, for example, has pointed out that Mills's

> projection of the concept of a triangular power elite, which he explicitly offers in preference to that of a ruling class, is based on a misconception of "ruling class." Moreover, in his tripartite division of the wielders of control he avoids comparing the relative weight of each of the three and tends to ignore the central depository of power—the financial overlords.[19]

This misconception of the *source* of power in American society prevented the development of a structural analysis of power linked to *class* until Domhoff introduced into the discussion the central role of the "upper class" in government through the former's transformation from a cohesive social-economic class into a "governing class," a topic we address in the next chapter.

Notes

1. See C. Wright Mills, *The Sociological Imagination* (New York: Oxford University Press, 1959); and idem, *The Power Elite* (New York: Oxford University Press, 1956). See also C. Wright Mills, *White Collar: The American Middle Classes* (New York: Oxford University Press, 1951).
2. Mills, *The Power Elite*, 277.
3. Ibid., 6, 9; emphasis added.
4. Ibid., 4.
5. C. Wright Mills, "The Structure of Power in American Society," in *Power, Politics, and People: The Collected Essays of C. Wright Mills*, ed. Irving Louis Horowitz (New York: Oxford University Press, 1963), 27.
6. Mills, *The Power Elite*, 276.
7. Mills, "The Structure of Power in American Society," 35.
8. Mills, *The Power Elite*, 275.
9. Ibid., 202.
10. Mills, "The Structure of Power in American Society," 28
11. Ibid.
12. Mills, *The Power Elite*, 219, 221–22.
13. Ibid., 222.
14. Ibid., 202.
15. Ibid.

16. See G. William Domhoff and Hoyt B. Ballard, eds. *C. Wright Mills and the Power Elite* (Boston: Beacon Press, 1969).

17. G. William Domhoff, *The Higher Circles: The Governing Class in America* (New York: Vintage, 1971), 139.

18. For an extended discussion on this point, see the next chapter.

19. Herbert Aptheker, *The World of C. Wright Mills* (New York: Marzani and Munsell, 1960), 19–20.

Chapter 13

DOMHOFF ON THE POWER STRUCTURE AND THE GOVERNING CLASS

Taking Mills's analysis of the American power structure one step further, G. William Domhoff has made an important contribution to our understanding of the social basis of political power by linking the upper class to the major political institutions of American society, especially the state—a relationship embodied in the concept of the "governing class."[1]

This chapter examines the ideas of Domhoff on the American power structure, which he, like Mills, developed as a critique of pluralist theory. Examining his analysis of the governing class in America, the chapter provides a critical overview of his concept of political power in America that goes beyond Mills's characterization of the power elite.

The Power Structure

In his now classic *Who Rules America?* Domhoff took a giant step forward beyond Mills's pioneering study of the power elite by looking behind the movers and shapers of American domestic and foreign policy. Attempting to understand the common interests of the leading forces of the power structure and their connection to the social upper class of wealthy owners of the giant corporations, Domhoff discovered that through a multitude of political processes the upper class has come directly and indirectly to dominate the government and has become a ruling, or governing, class.

Clarifying the meaning of the concepts of "power elite," "upper class," and "governing class," Domhoff makes explicit his own analysis of the Americal power structure and thus sets himself apart from that developed by Mills. The "power elite," Domhoff points out, "encompasses all those who are in command positions in institutions controlled by members of the upper (governing) class."[2] In this sense, Domhoff's definition of the power elite is similar to Mills's concept, that is, an elite made up of the top functionaries of the leading institutions of American society, but goes beyond Mills's tripartite model of power, in that Domhoff differentiates the position of the power elite from that of the upper class. Referring to the former, "This power elite," Domhoff argues, "is the *leadership group* of the upper class as a whole,"

> but it is *not the same thing as the upper class*, for not all members of the upper class are members of the power elite and not all members of the power elite are part of the upper class. It is members of the power elite who take part in the processes that maintain the class structure.[3]

What distinguishes Domhoff's approach from that of Mills is Domhoff's focus on the central problematic of "whether or not the institution [that the power elite serves] is *controlled by members of the upper class*,"[4] for it is this *class control* that is decisive, *not* the particular characteristics or motives of the power elite per se, as Mills had emphasized. "Thus, if we can show that members of the upper class," Domhoff continues,

> control the corporations through stock ownership and corporate directorships, the military through the Department of Defense, and the corporate law profession through large corporate law firms and major law schools, we will have gone a long way toward demonstrating that *the aims of the American power elite*, as defined by either Mills or this book, *are necessarily those of members of the upper class*.[5]

Domhoff defines the upper class as a social class "made up of rich businessmen and their families" and points out that it is

> closely knit by such institutions as stock ownership, trust funds, intermarriages, private schools, exclusive city clubs, exclusive summer resorts, debutante parties, foxhunts, charity drives, and, last but not least, corporation boards.[6]

In short, the upper class, Domhoff points out, is based on "great wealth and unique life styles of intermarrying and interacting families of high social standing."[7] After a detailed examination of the position and connections of the wealthy in America, Domhoff concludes: "There is in the United States an intermarrying social upper class, based upon business wealth, that has a rather definite set of boundaries which are guarded by . . . exclusive institutions."[8]

Going a step further, Domhoff raises the central question of his inquiry: "Is this social upper class, with its several institutional focal points and its several means of assimilating new members, also a 'governing class'?"[9] And, if so, what is the process by which the American upper class becomes a national governing class?

The Upper Class as Governing Class

In both *Who Rules America?* and *The Higher Circles: The Governing Class in America*, Domhoff documents how the upper class is in fact a cohesive social class based on the ownership of the large corporations and banks and that this class, through its control of numerous private and public institutions, has become a "governing class."[10] Defining the governing class as

> a social upper class which owns a disproportionate amount of the country's wealth, receives a disproportionate share of the country's yearly income, contributes a disproportionate number of its members to governmental bodies and decision-making groups, and dominates the policy-forming process through a variety of means[11]

Domhoff goes on to show how, through numerous institutional mechanisms, the social upper class becomes a bona fide governing class.

After extensive study and analysis of the relationship between the upper class, the power elite, and the key governmental institutions of American society, Domhoff concludes: "Members of the American upper class and their employees control the Executive branch of the federal government, . . . the Judicial branch and the regulatory agencies," including "the military, the CIA, and the FBI."[12] Moreover, the upper class is well represented in and has substantial influence over the legislative branch and has an impact on other key institutions, including universities, foundations, clubs, advisory councils, and numerous other organizations.[13] Through this control and domination of the key governmental and social institutions of American society, the upper class has become a governing class, according to Domhoff.

Whereas Domhoff had in his earlier work avoided the use of the term "ruling class" because, as he put it, it is "a term that implies a Marxist view of history"[14] (with which he apparently did not want to be identified), opting instead for "the more neutral term 'governing class,'"[15] in his later works—beginning with *The Powers That Be: Processes of Ruling Class Domination in America*—Domhoff drops the term "governing class" and substitutes in its place the concept of the "ruling class"—a concept he had rejected a decade earlier.[16]

In the opening chapter of *The Powers That Be*, titled "The Ruling Class and the Problem of Power," Domhoff defines the term "ruling class" as follows:

> By a ruling class I mean a clearly demarcated social class which has "power" over the government (state apparatus) and underlying population within a given nation (state). Evidence for the "power" of a ruling class can be found in such indicators as:
>
> 1. A disproportionate amount of wealth and income as compared to other social classes and groups within the state;
> 2. A higher standing than other social classes within the state on a variety of well-being statistics;
> 3. Control over the major social and economic institutions of the state;
> 4. Domination over the governmental processes of the country.[17]

In a broader sense, then, the "ruling class is a social class that subordinates other social classes to its own profit or advantage"[18] and dominates the major institutions of society, especially the state, to advance its class interests.

Differentiating his concept of the "ruling class" from Mills's "power elite," Domhoff writes: "C. Wright Mills first introduced the concept of a power elite into the sociological literature as a substitute for 'ruling class.'"[19]

> I define the power elite as the leadership group or *operating arm* of the ruling class. It is made up of active, working members of the ruling class and high-level employees in institutions controlled by members of the ruling class.[20]

"The difference between Mills' definition and mine," Domhoff continues, "lies in the fact that"

> (1) I do not assume *a priori* that any institutionally based group is by definition part of the power elite, as Mills did in so designating leaders within corporate, military and governmental bureaucracies; and (2) I have grounded the power elite in a social class. Using this approach, it is possible to determine empirically which parts of the economy and government can be considered direct outposts of the ruling class by virtue of disproportionate participation by members of the power elite.[21]

"Both of these concepts—ruling class and power elite," Domhoff concludes, "are important in an examination of how America is ruled, for they bring together the class-rule and institutional-elite perspectives" of power in American society.[22]

Conclusion

Despite his significant contribution to power-structure research and substantial improvement over Mills's concept of the power elite, Domhoff has been criticized for paying insufficient attention to class relations and class struggle beyond the instrumental identification of control of the state and other institutions of American society by the governing (or ruling) upper class. Marxist critics have faulted him for having focused too much on the institutional aspects of the policy-formation process and for ignoring a class analysis of the capitalist political economy that incorporates a dialectical approach to class. Moreover, Domhoff's loose usage of the term "upper class" has led to further criticism of his overall model, which he has built outside the Marxist problematic of the ruling *capitalist* class.

While Domhoff in his latest book, *The Power Elite and the State*, attempts to correct this shortcoming by injecting an element of class analysis into his new theory of power and the state, he, like Mills, continues to reject Marxist theories of the state and opts instead for an eclectic-empiricist approach in line with his previous studies of power in the United States.[23] Thus, although he clearly states that "the relationship between states and social classes [is] the crucial issue of this book," Domhoff criticizes the efforts of the structural Marxists by asserting that "they abandoned the study of social power in general for more narrow concerns such as 'class structure' or 'state power.'"[24] Rejecting the Marxist approach and anticipating criticisms of the eclectic theoretical position he has come to adopt in his studies of the U.S. power structure during the past twenty-five years, Domhoff admits:

> After all those years spent wandering in the empirical wilderness, surrounded on every side by pluralists, structural Marxists, and utility maximizers . . . I hope the eclecticism of my view . . . does not continue to create confusion for the pigeonholers, taxonomists, and single-cause theorists who now dominate discussions of power in America.[25]

Domhoff's objections to structural Marxism notwithstanding, to develop a more comprehensive understanding of the relationship between class, power, and the state, we turn in the next chapter to the debate on the theory of the capitalist state—a debate that has taken center stage in Marxist circles during the past two decades.

Notes

1. See G. William Domhoff, *Who Rules America?* (Englewood Cliffs, N.J.: Prentice Hall, 1967); and idem, *The Higher Circles: The Governing Class in America* (New York: Vintage, 1971).

For the relationship of Domhoff's work to that of Mills, see G. William Domhoff and Hoyt B. Ballard, eds., *C. Wright Mills and the Power Elite* (Boston: Beacon Press, 1968).

2. Domhoff, *Who Rules America?* 10.

3. G. William Domhoff, *Who Rules America Now?* (New York: Simon & Schuster, 1983), 2.

4. Domhoff, *Who Rules America?* 10; emphasis added.

5. Ibid.

6. Ibid., 4.

7. Domhoff, *The Higher Circles*, 32.

8. Domhoff, *Who Rules America?*, 33.

9. Ibid., 5.

10. See Domhoff, *The Higher Circles*, 103–9 and idem, *Who Rules America?* 156. See also G. William Domhoff, *The Powers That Be: The Processes of Ruling Class Domination in America* (New York: Vintage, 1979), chap. 1.

11. Domhoff, *The Higher Circles*, 109.

12. Domhoff, *Who Rules America?* 84, 131.

13. Domhoff, *Who Rules America Now?* chaps. 4 and 5.

14. Domhoff, *Who Rules America?* 3.

15. Ibid.

16. See Domhoff, *The Powers That Be*.

17. Ibid., 12.

18. Ibid., 13.

19. Ibid., 13–14.

20. Ibid. 13; emphasis added.

21. Ibid., 14.

22. Ibid., 14–15.

23. See G. William Domhoff, *The Power Elite and the State* (New York: Aldine de Gruyter, 1990).

24. Ibid., xviii, 7. Domhoff writes: "I believe that the Marxian analysis of the state in democratic capitalist societies is wrong because it incorporates a false homology between the economy and the state that distorts its view of the state and creates a tendency to downplay the importance of representative democracy." Ibid., 8.

25. Ibid., xix, 14–15.

Chapter 14

ALTHUSSER, POULANTZAS, AND MILIBAND ON POLITICS AND THE STATE

This chapter focuses on the views of three contemporary Marxist theorists—Louis Althusser, Nicos Poulantzas, and Ralph Miliband—on politics and the state in capitalist society. Concerned with the base-superstructure problematic and the nature and role of the capitalist state, these theorists provide us with the framework for an informed analysis of the debates on the state and politics in late capitalist society.

Ideology and the Political Superstructure

In the late 1960s, Louis Althusser reintroduced into Marxist discourse Lenin's and Gramsci's contributions on ideology and the state and provided an extended discussion on the basic concepts of historical materialism. Althusser played a key role in the effort to revitalize critical thought on the subject through the incorporation of the Gramscian notion of ideological hegemony into his own analysis of "ideological state apparatuses."[1]

In linking the political superstructure to the social-economic base, or mode of production, Althusser argued in favor of the classical Marxist position, which identifies the superstructure as determined "in the last instance" by the base: "The upper floors," he wrote, in reference to the political superstructure, "could not 'stay up' (in the air) alone, if they did not rest precisely on their base."[2] Thus the state, the supreme political institution and repressive apparatus of society, "enables the ruling classes to ensure their domination over the working class, thus enabling the former to subject the latter to the process of surplus-value extortion."[3] This is so precisely because the state is controlled by the ruling class. And such control makes the state, and the superstructure in general, dependent on, and determined by, the dominant class in the base.

In his essay "Ideology and Ideological State Apparatuses," Althusser expands his analysis of the base-superstructure relationship to include other superstructural institutions—cultural, religious, educational, legal, and so on.

As the hegemony of the ruling class in these spheres becomes critical for its control over the dominated classes, and society in general, the class struggle takes on a three-tiered attribute, consisting of the economic, political, and ideological levels. Central to the process of ruling-class ideological domination is the installation by the ruling class of the dominant ideology in the ideological state apparatuses, according to Althusser.

> The ideology of the ruling class does not become the ruling ideology by virtue of the seizure of state power alone. It is by the installation of the ideological state apparatuses in which this ideology is realized itself that it becomes the ruling ideology.[4]

The relationship between ruling-class domination and the dominant ideology is also emphasized by Poulantzas, who further developed Althusser's conceptualization of ideology, situating it in the context of class domination and class struggle. "The dominant ideology, by assuring the practical insertion of agents in the social structure," Poulantzas points out, "aims at the maintenance (the cohesion) of the structure, and this means *above all class* domination and exploitation."[5]

> It is precisely in this way that within a social formation ideology is dominated by the ensemble of representations, values, notions, beliefs, etc. by means of which class domination is perpetuated: in other words it is dominated by what can be called the ideology of the dominant class.[6]

This Althusserian conception of the relationship between the base and the superstructure, especially the state and the ideological state apparatuses, came to inform Poulantzas's analysis of classes, class struggle, and the state and set the stage for the recent discussion and debate on the Marxist theory of the state.

The Poulantzas-Miliband Debate on the Capitalist State

The Poulantzas-Miliband debate on the nature and role of the capitalist state in the early 1970s prompted renewed interest in Marxist theorizing on the capitalist state during the past two decades.[7] In this debate, one position emphasized the direct and indirect control of the state by the dominant capitalist class, and another emphasized the structural imperatives of the capitalist system affecting the state and its "relative autonomy." These two views correspond to the so-called "instrumentalist" and "structuralist" positions associated with Ralph Miliband and Nicos Poulantzas, respectively. Central to the debate are questions related to the class nature of the state, the relationship between different classes and the state, and the notion of relative autonomy in the exercise of state power.[8]

In his original formulation of the problem in *The State in Capitalist Society*, Miliband approaches the question of the state via a critique of the pluralist models still dominant in political sociology and mainstream political theory. In so doing, he provides an approach and analysis that earns his work the unwarranted label "instrumentalism." And it is in reaction to this instrumentalism that critiques of his work have resulted in the formulation of a counterposition that has come to be labeled "structuralism."

The central question addressed in the initial formulation of the instrumentalist problematic has been a determination of the role of the state in a society dominated by capitalist social relations. In this context, Miliband's study of the capitalist state focuses on the special relationship between the state and the capitalist class, and the mechanisms of control of the state by this class that de facto transform the state into a *capitalist state*.

In contrast, Poulantzas, representing the so-called structuralist position, focuses on the structural constraints of the capitalist system that set limits to the state's autonomy and force it to work within the framework of an order that yields results invariably favorable to the dominant capitalist class. According to this view, it is by virtue of the system of production itself in capitalist society that the state becomes a *capitalist* state, even in the absence of direct control of the state apparatus by capitalists.

It should be pointed out, however, that the degree of lack of direct control of the state apparatus by the capitalist class determines the degree of the state's relative autonomy from this class. And this relative autonomy in turn gives the state the necessary freedom to manage the overall interests of the capitalist class and rule society on behalf of the established capitalist order.

The central problem for these competing views of the state is not so much whether the state in capitalist society is a *capitalist* state—they agree that it is—but *how* that state *becomes* a capitalist state. Far more than the limited academic value, the answers to this question have immense political implications because the debates surrounding this issue originally emerged in Europe in response to the pivotal political question regarding the strategy and tactics of taking state power under advanced capitalism.

Instrumentalism versus Structuralism

Let us briefly look at the fundamentals of the instrumentalist versus structuralist problematic and show, in the process, that the dichotomy has been ill conceived, as both Miliband and Poulantzas ultimately, in later reformulation of their positions, basically accept the validity of their critics' conclusions.

To start with, in his initial formulation of the problem, Miliband writes:

> In the Marxist scheme, the "ruling class" of capitalist society is that class which owns and controls the means of production and which is able, by virtue of the economic power thus conferred upon it, to use the state as its instrument for the domination of society.[9]

This seemingly instrumentalist statement is expounded by Miliband through his focus on "patterns and consequences of personal and social ties between individuals occupying positions of power in different institutional spheres."[10] Concentrating on a study of the nature of the capitalist class, the mechanisms that tie this class to the state, and the specific relationships between state policies and class interests,[11] Miliband leaves himself open to charges of voluntarism and instrumentalism.

In contrast, Poulantzas argues that "the direct participation of members of the capitalist class in the state apparatus and in the government, even where it exists, is not the important side of the matter."[12] What is crucial to understand, according to Poulantzas, is this:

> The relation between the bourgeois class and the state is an *objective relation*. This means that if the *function* of the state in a determinate social formation and the *interests* of the dominant class in this formation *coincide*, it is by reason of the system itself: the direct participation of members of the ruling class in the state apparatus is not the cause but the *effect*, and moreover a chance and contingent one, of this objective coincidence.[13]

In this formulation, the functions of the state are broadly determined by the structural imperatives of the capitalist mode of production and the constraints placed on it by the structural environment in which the state must operate. Given these parameters of operation, the state obtains relative autonomy from the various fractions of the capitalist class in order to carry out its functions as a capitalist state. Thus Poulantzas accepts the control of the state by the capitalist class through direct or indirect means or both, but assigns to it relative autonomy vis-à-vis any one *fraction* of that class.[14] Hence, in this formulation, the capitalist state is the state of the capitalist class and serves the interests of that class as a whole; and at the same time it maintains relative autonomy from its various fractions.

Convergence of the Two Views

Miliband, defending himself against vulgar instrumentalist interpretations of his argument, later concedes that the state can and must have a certain degree of autonomy from the capitalist class. Referring to Marx and Engels's assertion that "the modern state is but a committee for managing the common affairs of the whole bourgeoisie," Miliband writes:

> This has regularly been taken to mean not only that the state acts *on behalf* of the dominant class . . . but that it acts *at the behest* of that class which is an altogether different assertion and, as I would argue, a vulgar deformation of the thought of Marx and Engels. . . . [T]he notion of common affairs assumes the existence of particular ones; and the notion of the whole bourgeoisie implies the existence of separate elements which make up that whole. This being the case, there is an obvious need for an institution of the kind they refer to, namely the state; and the state *cannot* meet this need without enjoying a certain degree of autonomy. In other words, the notion of autonomy is embedded in the definition itself, is an intrinsic part of it.[15]

Elsewhere, Miliband addresses this question more directly: "Different forms of state have different degrees of autonomy. But all states enjoy some autonomy or independence from all classes, including the dominant classes."[16] Nevertheless,

> the relative independence of the state does not reduce its class character: on the contrary, its relative independence makes it *possible* for the state to play its class role in an appropriately flexible manner. If it really was the simple "instrument" of the "ruling class," it would be fatally inhibited in the performance of its role.[17]

He goes on to argue that:

> the intervention of the state is always and necessarily partisan: as a class state, it always intervenes for the purpose of maintaining the existing system of domination, even where it intervenes to mitigate the harshness of that system of domination.[18]

Thus Miliband takes a big step toward reconciliation with the relative autonomy thesis while retaining the core of his argument in seeing the capitalist state as an institution controlled by the capitalist class as a whole.

Poulantzas, in his later writings, also moves in a direction away from his earlier position on relative autonomy. He admits that in the current monopoly stage of capitalism, the *monopoly fraction* of the capitalist class dominates the state and thereby secures favorable policies in its own favor over other fractions of the bourgeois power bloc.[19] This situation, he adds, poses problems to the state's traditional role as "political organizer of the general interest of the bourgeoisie" and "restrict[s] the limits of the relative autonomy of the state in relation to monopoly capital and to the field of the compromises it makes with other fractions of the bourgeoisie."[20] The political crisis resulting from this fractional domination and fragmentation, argues Poulantzas, leads to a crisis of the bourgeois state.[21]

Conclusion

With these later reformulations of state theory by both Poulantzas and Miliband, we see a convergence of the two positions and arrive at the general conclusion that the state in capitalist society is both controlled by and, simultaneously, relatively autonomous of the various fractions of the capitalist class, in order to (1) perform its functions in advancing the interests of the capitalist class as a whole, and at the same time (2) maintain its legitimacy over society. This "relative autonomy," however, is rapidly being undermined by the hegemonic (monopoly) fraction of the capitalist class, which as a result is blocking the state's effectiveness in fulfilling its political role as the "executive committee" of the entire bourgeoisie.

More recently, some neo-Weberian theorists have introduced an alternative, "state-centered" approach that grants greater (not less) autonomy to the state and views state managers as autonomous agents who are independent of the prevailing class structure in society. We provide a critical analysis of this approach in the next chapter.

Notes

1. See Louis Althusser, *For Marx* (London: Penguin, 1969); and idem, *Lenin and Philosophy and Other Essays* (New York: Monthly Review Press, 1971). See also Louis Althusser and Etienne Balibar, *Reading Capital* (London: New Left Books, 1970).

2. Althusser, *Lenin and Philosophy and Other Essays*, 135.

3. Ibid., 137.

4. Ibid., 185.

5. Nicos Poulantzas, *Political Power and Social Classes* (London: New Left Books, 1974), 209.

6. Ibid.

7. The debate began with a review of Ralph Miliband's *The State in Capitalist Society* (London: Basic Books, 1969) by Nicos Poulantzas, "The Problem of the Capitalist State," *New Left*

Review, no. 58 (1969), to which Miliband responded in the next issue of the same journal. See Ralph Miliband, "The Capitalist State—Reply to Nicos Poulantzas," *New Left Review*, no. 59 (1970). See also Nicos Poulantzas, *Political Power and Social Classes* (London: New Left Books, 1974); Ralph Miliband, "Poulantzas and the Capitalist State," *New Left Review*, no. 82 (1973); and Nicos Poulantzas, "The Capitalist State: A Reply to Miliband and Laclau," *New Left Review*, no. 95 (1976). Among Poluantzas's later works, see *Classes in Contemporary Capitalism* (London: New Left Books, 1975) and *State, Power, Socialism* (London: New Left Books, 1978). Miliband's subsequent arguments can be found in his "Political Forms and Historical Materialism," in *Socialist Register*, ed. R. Miliband and J. Saville (London: Merlin Press, 1975) and *Marxism and Politics* (London: Oxford University Press, 1977).

8. See David Gold, Clarence Y.H. Lo, and Erik Olin Wright, "Some Recent Developments in Marxist Theories of the Capitalist State," pts. 1 and 2, *Monthly Review* (October and November 1975); Gosta Esping-Andersen, Roger Friedland, and Erik Olin Wright, "Modes of Class Struggle and the Capitalist State," *Kapitalistate*, nos. 4–5 (Summer 1976); Albert Szymanski, *The Capitalist State and the Politics of Class* (Cambridge, Mass.: Winthrop, 1978); Bob Jessop, *The Capitalist State* (New York: New York University Press, 1982); Martin Carnoy, *The State and Political Theory* (Princeton: Princeton University Press, 1984).

9. Miliband, *The State in Capitalist Society*, 23.

10. Gold, Lo, and Wright, "Marxist Theories of the Capitalist State," 33.

11. Ibid., 32–33.

12. Poulantzas, "Problem of the Capitalist State," 73.

13. Ibid.

14. Poulantzas, *Political Power*; and idem, *State, Power, Socialism*.

15. Miliband, "Poulantzas and the Capitalist State," 85.

16. Miliband, *Marxism and Politics*, 83.

17. Ibid., 87.

18. Ibid., 91.

19. Nicos Poulantzas, "The Political Crisis and the Crisis of the State," in *Critical Sociology: European Perspectives*, ed. J.W. Freiberg (New York: Irvington, 1979), 374–81.

20. Ibid., 375.

21. Ibid., 357–93.

Chapter 15

TRIMBERGER, BLOCK, AND SKOCPOL AND NEO-WEBERIAN THEORIZING

This chapter examines a number of contemporary attempts in neo-Weberian theorizing on the state and society by theorists influenced by the Weberian school—Ellen Kay Trimberger, Fred Block, and Theda Skocpol. Providing a political theory of state-society relations, these theorists stress the autonomy of the state vis-à-vis the dominant and dominated classes and characterize the state as a source of power independent of the contending class forces.[1]

In what follows we present a critical analysis of the main arguments advanced by these theorists and contrast their views to the Marxist theory of the state discussed in the previous chapter.

Autonomous Bureaucrats and Political Power

Ellen Kay Trimberger, in her book *Revolution from Above*, attempts to develop a neo-Weberian theory of the state and society, arguing that the state should be seen as playing an independent role and state bureaucrats as independent agents free of class control. "A bureaucratic state apparatus, or a segment of it can be said to be relatively autonomous," Trimberger writes, "when those who hold high civil and/or military posts satisfy two conditions":

> (1) They are not recruited from the dominant landed, commercial or industrial classes; and (2) they do not form close personal and economic ties with these classes after their elevation to high office. Relatively autonomous bureaucrats are thus independent of those classes which control the means of production.[2]

Trimberger goes on to argue that "dynamically autonomous bureaucrats enter the class struggle as an *independent* force, rather than as an instrument of other class forces."[3] Going a step further, she contends that these bureaucrats "have a distinctive class position" and that they can "use their control over state resources—coercive, monetary, and ideological—to destroy the existing economic and class order."[4] Moreover:

> even in polities where the state bureaucracy is subordinate to a party and parliamentary system controlled by [dominant] class interests . . . , relatively autonomous military officers have the potential for breaking this institutional subordination by force.[5]

If, as Trimberger contends, these "autonomous" bureaucrats hold on to no particular class interests of their own (or those of other classes), it is not clear why they would be "acting to destroy an existing economic and class order" in crisis situations.[6] What Trimberger fails to tell us is (1) the class ideology of these bureaucrats (which is substantially, but not exclusively, determined by their class origin); (2) the class interests they intend to serve (which is related to the above considerations of origin, ideology, or both), and, most important, (3) the structural consequences of policies pursued by these bureaucrats and their positive or negative impact on different classes.

Trimberger's general contention that "control of the governing apparatus is a source of power independent of that held by class"[7] constitutes a departure from the Marxist theory of the state discussed in the previous chapter. She confirms this departure by stating that

> neither the Marxist nor the non-Marxist political sociology of Third World societies has looked at the relationship between the state apparatus and dominant classes as an *independent* variable determining the type and rate of change in the transition from agrarian to industrial societies.[8]

In this sense, the approach taken by Trimberger on this issue is in effect a restatement of a revised version of the Weberian position.

State Managers and Power Politics

An extension of this line of reasoning has led other theorists in a pluralist direction where, as evidenced in Fred Block's argument, the state and state officials become "autonomous agents," so that they acquire independence from the capitalist class and, further, determine policy over the heads of this class, including the formulation of policies that sometimes go against the interests of the capitalists as a whole.[9]

In his controversial article "The Ruling Class Does Not Rule," Block attacks the structuralist position of Poulantzas as "a slightly more sophisticated version" of instrumentalism and proposes to replace it with his own reformulation of the problem. The underlying argument advanced by Block against the structuralist-instrumentalist problematic discussed in the previous chapter rests on his conception of the role of "state managers," who, according to Block, are autonomous agents functioning in their own self (or positional) interests and are not consciously engaged in the protection of the interests of the capitalist class as such. Thus, Block introduces into the debate "autonomous state managers" controlled by no one and subservient to no particular class interests other than their own—although they are forced to formulate policies within the framework of an environment that includes both capitalist domination of the economy and class struggle between the two contending class forces, the capitalists and the workers. This becomes clear when Block states: "State managers do have an interest in expanding their own power, including their own power to manage the economy."[10] To back up this claim, Block writes: "German capitalists were reduced to being functionaries, albeit highly paid functionaries, of the Nazi state that was acting in its own profoundly irrational interests."[11]

Elsewhere, Block asserts that "the rationality of the capitalist state emerges out of the three-sided relationship between state managers, capital and subordinate classes."[12] Referring to his own theoretical formulation, and distancing himself from Marxism, he writes:

> The virtue of this model is that it allows one to get away from the standard Marxist methodological tool of assuming that state policies always reflect the intentionality of a social class or sector of a class. It renders obsolete the procedure of looking for a specific social base for any particular state policy.[13]

He goes on to assert:

> One can say that a policy objectively benefited a particular social class, but that is very different from saying that this social class, or sector of a class, subjectively wanted the policy or that its intentions were a critical element in policy development.[14]

This leads him to conclude: "The road to analytic confusion in Marxism is paved with an exaggerated concern with class intentionality."[15]

Block's critique of Marxism, for its "narrow focus on 'class struggles,'" has during the past decade taken him down what he calls a "Post-Marxist" path, rejecting historical materialism altogether. In his recent book *Revising State Theory* Block continues to see the state as an autonomous agent, arguing that politics is "irreducible" and that social struggles, such as those around race and gender, cannot be explained as manifestations of class struggle.[16] Advocating a position that would "go beyond Marxism," Block asserts: "The answers that Marx offered no longer suffice, and just as Marx sought to transcend Hegel, so too, those who pursue the Post-Marxist project seek to transcend Marx."[17] This, he feels, would free him to introduce into his analysis

> many other collective actors organized around race, gender, age, sexual orientation, religious orientation, or shared views about the environment or the arms race. In place of a narrow focus on "class struggles," the emphasis would be on a broad range of social struggles.[18]

Block's seemingly "broader" reformulation of state theory, which allows state managers considerable autonomy while bringing in a multitude of social actors beyond classes, unfortunately turns out to be a "slightly more sophisticated version" of recent neo-Weberian approaches than a new attempt at a reconstruction of prevailing Marxist theories of the state and society.

Class, State, and Society: A "State-Centered" Approach

Other neo-Weberian theorists, like Theda Skocpol, have adopted an approach similar to that of Trimberger and Block in conceptualizing the state as an independent force, and in the process have come to embrace a more elaborate "state-centered" approach, rejecting the Marxist position on the class nature of the state.[19] Influenced by Weberian theory, Skocpol in her book *States and Social Revolutions* attempts to counter the classical Marxist position on the relationship of the state to the mode of production and the class basis of politics and the state.[20] She writes:

> In contrast to most (especially recent) Marxist theories, this view refuses to treat states as if they were mere analytic aspects of abstractly conceived modes of production, or even political aspects of concrete class relations and struggles. Rather it insists that states are actual organizations controlling (or attempting to control) territories and people.[21]

Arguing in favor of the view that the state is an entity with "an autonomous structure—a structure with a logic and interests of its own,"[22] Skocpol examines the French, Russian, and Chinese revolutions in terms of the centrality of the state's role in "acting for itself." Adopting an "organizational" and "realist" perspective on the state,[23] "state and party organizations," she argues, must be viewed "as *independent* determinants of political conflicts and outcomes."[24] Thus, for Skocpol "the state organizations . . . have a more central and autonomous place" because, like Trimberger and Block, she sees in the state "potential autonomy of action over . . . the dominant class and existing relations of production."[25]

In this reformulation of the class-state problematic, the state is divorced from and opposed to existing social classes and acts in accordance with its distinct interests, based primarily on the maintenance of internal order and competition against external forces (i.e., other states) threatening its survival.

> The state normally performs two basic sets of tasks: It maintains order, and it competes with other actual or potential states. . . . [T]he state's own fundamental interest in maintaining sheer physical order and political peace may lead it—especially in periods of crisis—to enforce concessions to subordinate-class demands. These concessions may be at the expense of the interests of the dominant class, but not contrary to the state's own interests in controlling the population and collecting taxes and military recruits.[26]

Thus:

> If state organizations cope with whatever tasks they already claim smoothly and efficiently, legitimacy . . . will probably be accorded to the state's form and rulers by most groups in society. . . . Loss of legitimacy, especially among the crucial [politically powerful] groups, tends to ensue with a vengeance if and when . . . the state fails consistently to cope with existing tasks, or proves unable to cope with new tasks suddenly thrust upon it by crisis circumstances.[27]

"The political crises that have launched social revolutions," writes Skocpol, "have not at all been epiphenomenal reflections of societal strains or class contradictions. Rather, they have been direct expressions of contradictions centered in the structures of old-regime states."[28] Thus, to understand better those processes by which the state has taken center stage of history, Skocpol suggests "the need for a more state-centered approach" in studying states and social revolutions.[29]

Some Concluding Observations

Contrary to the Trimberger, Block, and Skocpol formulations, one could argue that although the state can, and sometimes does, gain limited autonomy from the direct control of main class forces in society (especially during periods of crises), this autonomy by no means implies the class neutrality of the state and its agents, that the state and state officials are "above class."

Clearly, the state cannot be seen in terms distinct from class forces and class struggles in society. However independent it may at times *appear* to be, the state, as the supreme superstructural institution in society, is in the final analysis a reflection of the underlying mode of production defined by definite relations of production that characterize the class nature of that state.

This understanding of the materialist dynamics of history lies at the heart of Marx's class analysis which we discussed at the beginning of this book. In the final, closing pages of this book we return to this theme once again, where a more complete understanding of the relationship between the state and society will be explored, and the real nature of politics and the state revealed.

Before returning to historical materialism and class analysis, however, we take up in the next few chapters other important theories that address aspects of society and social relations characteristic of life under contemporary capitalism.

Notes

1. See E.K. Trimberger, *Revolution from Above: Military Bureaucrats and Development in Japan, Turkey, and Peru* (New Brunswick, N.J.: Transaction Books, 1978); Theda Skocpol, *States and Revolutions: A Comparative Analysis of France, Russia and China* (Cambridge, England: Cambridge University Press, 1979); Fred Block, "The Ruling Class Does Not Rule: Notes on the Marxist Theory of the State," *Socialist Review*, no. 33 (May–June 1977).
2. Trimberger, *Revolution from Above*, 4.
3. Ibid., 5; emphasis added.
4. Ibid., 4.
5. Ibid.
6. Ibid., 4–5.
7. Ibid., 7.
8. Ibid., 8.
9. See Block, "The Ruling Class Does Not Rule"; and idem, "Class Consciousness and Capitalist Rationalization: A Reply to Critics," *Socialist Review*, nos. 40–41 (July–October 1978).
10. Ibid., 40–41.
11. Ibid., 219.
12. Fred Block, "Marxist Theories of the State in World System Analysis," paper presented at the First Annual Political Economy of the World System Conference, American University, Washington, D.C., March–April 1977, 8.
13. Ibid.
14. Ibid.
15. Ibid.
16. Fred Block, *Revising State Theory* (Philadelphia: Temple University Press, 1987), 17–18, 34–35.

17. Ibid., 35.
18. Ibid., 18.

19. In acknowledging the affinity of his approach to state theory to Skocpol's "state-centered" approach, which we discuss later in the chapter, Block writes: "The systematization of a state-centered approach in the work of Theda Skocpol has been the other important new development in state theory. Skocpol has energetically argued that both the liberal and the Marxist traditions have been society-centered, explaining what goes on in the state as a function of what goes on in society. Her alternative is a state-centered approach that would provide a corrective to the standard view by stressing the diverse ways in which the state structures social life." Ibid., 20.

20. Skocpol, *States and Social Revolutions*. For an acknowledgment of this and other influences on Skocpol's views, see ibid., 301, notes 73 and 77.

21. Ibid., 31.

22. Ibid., 27. In developing this view of the state, Skocpol cites the works of Trimberger and Block, among others, and states: "I have been very greatly influenced by these writings, and by personal conversations with Trimberger and Block." Ibid., 301, note 73.

23. Ibid., 31.

24. Theda Skocpol, "Political Response to Capitalist Crisis: Neo-Marxist Theories of the State and the Case of the New Deal," *Politics and Society* 10, no. 2 (1981): 199.

25. Skocpol, *States and Social Revolutions*, 31.

26. Ibid., 30.

27. Ibid., 31–32.

28. Ibid., 29.

29. Ibid.

Chapter 16

GOFFMAN AND GARFINKEL ON DRAMATURGY, ETHNOMETHODOLOGY, AND EVERYDAY LIFE*

This chapter examines two "sociologies of everyday life," *dramaturgy* and *ethnomethodology*, as represented in the writings of Erving Goffman and Harold Garfinkel, respectively. These are, in a sense, social behaviorist approaches in that their prime concern is with detailing human behavior at the interpersonal level, as distinct from historical, comparative, or structural analysis of society and social relations.

Goffman and Self Presentation

A leading influence among social psychologists and the principal spokesperson for symbolic interactionism's dramaturgical approach was Erving Goffman. Influenced by Kenneth Burke's use of the dramaturgical metaphor, Goffman's early work is built on a single and simple premise: When people interact with each other, they do so through the use of symbolic devices that they employ in an attempt to "manage" the impressions others receive from them. The fact that Goffman preferred to treat life as a theater in which we stage, or "put on," shows for one another is made evident in his first major book *The Presentation of Self in Everyday Life*. In it he informs us:

> The perspective employed in this report is that of the theatrical performance; the principles derived are dramaturgical ones. I shall consider the way . . . the individual . . . presents himself and his activity to others, the ways in which he guides and controls the impressions they form of him, and the kinds of things he may and may not do while sustaining his performance before them.[1]

An examination of Goffman's early work clearly reveals that he conceptualized human social behavior as a series of "performances" by "actors" who

*This chapter was written by Larry T. Reynolds and Nancy J. Herman.

strive to present themselves (who "give" and "give off" "expressions" designed to create an "impression") as being exactly who and what they claim to be. Social behavior is a performance whose ultimate aim is to convince others of the authenticity of one's self. Operating either solo or in concert with their fellow actors and actresses as a team of players, people "stage shows" or "give performances" during which they "read social scripts," "enact routines," and "play parts" that utilize "props" and "settings." These performances are given in "front regions," which is to say before an "audience." The performances are "prepared" in society's "back regions." During these moments of preparation, when one is not "on stage," opportunities arise for anticipating whether one's performance will be well or ill received by the intended audience. The end product of a performance is the audience's "imputation" of a particular kind of self to the "character" being performed.[2]

The Presentation of Self in Everyday Life is not the only work in which one may catch the general flavor of Goffman's dramaturgical orientation. A fairly representative set of his ideas is contained in his book *Interaction Ritual: Essays in Face-to-Face Behavior*.[3] Here he deals with the fact that individuals interact so as to maintain both their own "face" and that of the other party(ies) involved in the interaction. In this work he also deals with the nature of deference and demeanor, with embarrassment, with alienation, with mental symptoms and tacit rules, and with the deliberate taking of avoidable risks in interaction.

Goffman's contribution to sociological theory in general and symbolic interactionism in particular goes beyond the application of his dramaturgical framework. In *Asylums: Essays on the Social Situation of Mental Patients and Other Inmates*, he makes an important contribution to the "labeling perspective" favored by many interactionists.[4] Goffman here applies the same social psychological analysis that appears in *The Presentation of Self in Everyday Life*. In studying mental patients, TB patients, military recruits, prisoners, and cloistered monks and nuns, Goffman coined the term "total institution"—places of work, residence, and confinement where large numbers of similarly defined individuals were physically and symbolically separated from the outside world. This separation had profound negative implications for self and identity. In such institutions, large numbers of persons are subjected to a regimented schedule. All aspects of their lives are conducted without privacy in the same locations under the supervisory body of the institution. As Goffman sees it, total institutions, through their rules, regulations, procedures and treatment of the inmates, function to humiliate and degrade individuals. Such structures serve to strip away the patient's/recruit's/novice's sense of dignity and self-worth and reduce them to total dependency on the hierarchical powers of the institution.[5]

Speaking of this process as "mortification of self," Goffman states that once in a total institution, it is virtually impossible to maintain positive, non-deviant self-images and identities. Individuals are physically separated from those on the outside who validate such identities and self-conceptions. Self is stripped through a number of procedures: individuals are often physically stripped of their clothing, belongings, jewelry, money, and other personal items—important components of their "identity kit." Moreover, they may be bathed, given a haircut, and issued institutional clothing. In so doing, they resemble all others in the institution. More importantly, they are proffered a new identity, as "mental patient," "army recruit," "prisoner," etc.—an identity that is reinforced on a daily basis by staff and other inmates alike. Through the entire structure of the total institution with its rewards and punishments, individuals gradually come to accept their new definition of self and its corresponding role and status.[6]

In a second study, *Stigma: Notes on the Management of Spoiled Identity*, Goffman considers the presentation of self by a number of persons, including minorities, ex-psychiatric patients, prisoners, the obese, the blind, and little people, etc. and how they manage their "spoiled identities."[7] For Goffman, all of these persons possess a stigma—a characteristic or attribute that is considered by society as a deviation from normalcy. Goffman defines three basic types of stigma: (1) abominations of the body, which include various physical deformities, such as a person missing limbs; (2) blemishes of individual character, qualities or actions influentially based on the individual having engaged in acts such as drug use, swinging, homosexuality, mental illness, etc. (3) tribal stigmas—stigmas of race, religion and nation. Regardless of the type, all stigmata denote individuals' spoiled identities; they are disvalued and conceived of as undesirable in the eyes of others.[8]

Goffman makes the distinction between "discredited" and "discreditable" identities. In terms of the former, individuals possess stigmas that are either readily apparent or known to others. Paraplegics, a woman with a seeing-eye dog, an obese man all possess discredited identities in Goffman's view. In terms of the latter, some individuals possess stigmas that are not readily apparent or known to others. Consider the case of the impotent male, the infertile female, a hermaphrodite or a former psychiatric patient—their deviant attributes are not obvious to others. Such persons, then, possess discreditable deviant identities.

Goffman contends that it is a continual effort on the part of both the discredited and the discreditable to attempt to manage such information about themselves. To be sure, deviants expend a great deal of time and energy at this never-ending task. As strategists, negotiators and expert managers, such persons employ a number of stratagems and techniques to mitigate the stigma of their "failing" on their daily rounds. Such stratagems include: deviance disavowal (normalization), total concealment, selective concealment, therapeutic disclosure, and preventive disclosure.[9]

But while Goffman has indeed made a major contribution to symbolic interactionism, it should be noted that his later work has tended to move in a different direction. His book *Frame Analysis: An Essay on the Organization of Experience* clearly departs from the central concerns of most interactionists.[10] In fact, feeling that Goffman's later work is best characterized as structuralism rather than interactionism, George Gonos notes that "Goffman's work stands opposed to the central tenets and most basic assumptions of symbolic interactionism."[11]

In *Frame Analysis*, Goffman is out to examine not impression management but life's microstructures. He no longer feels bound by W. I. Thomas's dictum that situations defined as real maybe real in their consequences. As Goffman sees things, "Defining situations as real certainly has consequences, but these may contribute very marginally to the events in progress."[12] Furthermore, he apparently has come to think that people seldom come up with new definitions of the situation on their own. Instead, they simply avail themselves of the definitions that "society" has provided.

The main thrust of *Frame Analysis* is "to isolate some of the basic frameworks of understanding available in our society for making sense out of events and to analyze the special vulnerabilities to which these frames of reference are subject."[13] Here Goffman has come to the position that sees human behavior as a product of simple adherence to society's rules and regulations. This view is, of course, anathema to most symbolic interactionists, as they favor a creative and less reactive picture of human action. This may, in part, account for the fact that while Goffman's works are indeed read by symbolic interactionists, he has, of late, attracted few interactionists to his banner. Furthermore, his later writings have come under fire by such well-known symbolic interactionists as Herbert Blumer and Norman K. Denzin. In fact, as very few interactionists would today identify themselves as dramaturgists, the dramaturgical approach may not remain a major variant of symbolic interactionism much longer. As it consistently either ignores or inadequately treats such issues as social class, social power, and social structure, its demise may be difficult to lament.[14]

Garfinkel and Ethnomethodology

While ethnomethodology can be said to have its precursors, its evolution is somewhat unlike that of most other theories. It really did not "take off" as a school of thought until it was given a name by UCLA sociologist Harold Garfinkel.[15] Emerging out of phenomenology, Garfinkel's ethnomethodology seeks to understand the methods people employ to make sense out of their worlds. It seeks to uncover the taken-for-granted assumptions underlying social interaction. Commonplace activities are characterized by an implicit order that occurs during the course of the interaction itself. This order serves to make our social situations "accountable," to use Garfinkel's term. For him, ethnomethodological studies "analyze everyday activities as members' methods for making those same activities visibly-rational-and-reportable-for-all-practical-purposes, that is, 'accountable' as organizations of commonplace activities."[16]

By the ethnomethodologists' reasoning, the assumptions of sociology are no different than the taken-for-granted assumptions made by nonsociologists in the course of carrying out their everyday activities. And ethnomethodology is, above all, concerned with, "the ways in which shared meanings . . . come to be taken for granted in human society."[17] As Paul Filmer et al. note, "sociology is, in an important sense, itself an everyday activity."[18] Thus, in approaching sociology as a form of everyday activity, and in seeking to explain that activity, the ethnomethodologists were led to look at sociology's own taken-for-granted assumptions. That, in itself, may be enough to occasion mainstream sociology's "contemptuous rejection" of ethnomethodology, but their questioning of one sociological assumption in particular is almost enough to guarantee it. That assumption is the assumption of order, and the way it is handled by the ethnomethodologists tells us something about ethnomethodology as a perspective.

As Nicolaus Mullins informs us, ethnomethodologists do not even directly examine the various manifestations of social order—such as social structure and social organization—they focus instead "on the process by which members manage to produce and sustain *a sense of social structure*."[19] For ethnomethodology "social order [is] a convenient fiction people allow each other to entertain so that mutual activity can proceed."[20]

Garfinkel argues that social order, or social reality, is not something that is simply "out there." Social realities "emerge relative to our particular position in social and cultural matrixes"; hence, "exactly *what* system of reality is defined as warranting our trust varies." These assumed realities "come to define . . . the ways in which the relationships themselves are interpreted and carried out during interaction."[21]

The ethnomethodologists, then, are concerned with the methods employed by both sociologists and nonsociologists, by the observer and the observed alike, in constructing their everyday realities. If the sociologists' constructed realities differ too greatly from the constructed realities of their subjects, or if sociologists fail to realize that their realities too are simply constructions, or social products, the process of understanding will be impeded.

We need to know "how people go about constructing in their own minds and conversations a view of the social world around them," write Randall Collins and Michael Makowsky: "People act as if reality were solid, given, and unambiguous, but the social world they communicate about is actually fluid, highly subject to interpretation, and not easily discoverable."[22] Thus, as Garfinkel points out, to develop an understanding of the meaning of people's everyday activities, ethnomethodologists set themselves the task of analyzing social situations in which people interact:

> Their study is directed to the tasks of learning how members' actual, ordinary activities consist of methods to make practical actions, practical circumstances, common sense knowledge of social structures, and practical sociological reasoning analyzable.[23]

In order to approach such "practical activity in everyday life," Garfinkel and other ethnomethodologists employ a variety of concepts such as "reflexivity," "accounting," "practical reasoning," "typification," and "documentary interpretation" in an attempt to disclose:

> (1) the nature of and extent to which various orders of meanings are *carried* in ordinary and common everyday exchanges of utterances, (2) the *underlying sense of meaning* tacitly accepted yet ordinarily unacknowledged by members involved in communication, (3) the *exchange* of intersubjectively meaningful *understanding* derived from communication, and (4) the nature of everyday exchanges as they constitute for members a sense of *rational, rule-like character* and thus are seen by members as making "sense".[24]

How, in short, can the commonplace be made visible? Garfinkel replies: "Procedurally it is my preference to start with familiar scenes and ask what can be done to make trouble."[25] This approach is aimed at achieving a better understanding of commonsense knowledge and behavior by first rendering them problematic. Only by disrupting the "routine" are the very taken-for-granted assumptions that make the social world a routine place more clearly revealed.

By Garfinkel's reasoning, there is more than one objective world and more than one "correct" way of structuring it: "The question is not one of what is the objective world and what is objective knowledge, but what are the varieties of objective knowledge."[26]

What Garfinkel seeks is to shake people up, to unsettle their daily routines and in the process of watching them putting their "lives back together" and "their houses back in order" to unearth and better understand the very processes by which social realities are constructed and social worlds rendered intelligible in the first place. In Garfinkel's words, "under the breach of the expectancies of everyday life, given the conditions for the optimal production of disturbance, persons should shift in exhibited confusion in an amount that is coordinate with the original extent of their grasp of the 'natural facts of life'."[27]

Garfinkel argues that people's adherence to society's rules "is not necessarily a product of their value commitments or belief in such rules. It may merely be . . . the anticipatory anxiety that prevents him from permitting a situation to develop, let alone confronting a situation, in which he has the alternative of acting or not with respect to a rule."[28] People may, then, fail to challenge rules, to break rules, to change rules, not because of a belief in the essential correctness of the rules, but because fear and anxiety prevent them from doing so. Much of our knowledge of the "rules" confers on these selfsame rules a character that has never been submitted to any test, and as Garfinkel points out, "the more important the rule, the greater is the likelihood that knowledge is based on avoided tests."[29] The implication here being that "insofar as the sociologist ignores this—that fear, anxiety, and ignorance, not positive value commitments, often account for compliance—he makes real persons in society into judgmental dopes."[30] One does not have to agree with Garfinkel's implicit image of people being little more than "blundering fools" in order to see that he has touched bedrock with his critique of conventional sociology's "over-socialized conception" of human nature. But as Zeitlin notes, in speaking of one of Garfinkel's studies:

> This experiment, and the principle it illustrates, has more implications than Garfinkel explicitly draws out; it has critical and even revolutionary implications in that it points directly to the potential flexibility, contingency, and changeability of institutions. It brings out clearly that institutions often regarded as necessary are merely those whose necessity has not been tested.[31]

Garfinkel's failure to spell out in detail the most radical implications of his findings is a characteristic shared by many ethnomethodologists. In some cases this reluctance may be a product of the belief that common-sense, everyday, knowledge, is "adequate and valid, with nothing more to be said about it."[32] It may also, in part, be a result of the fact that much of Garfinkel's ethnomethodology focuses on those microscopic features of social reality whose political implications for the larger social world are especially difficult to ascertain. Ignoring society's larger structural features comes at a price. In our opinion, that price is too high.

Conclusion

In this chapter we have glimpsed the strengths and weaknesses of the dramaturgical and ethnomethodological approaches by focusing on the works of Goffman and Garfinkel. On the positive side of the ledger, both perspectives detail the richness of social life in concrete social settings. They allow sociologists to "feel close" to their human subjects—to see things as they see them. On the ledger's other side, the microscopic, astructural aspects of both orientations not only result in an inadequate treatment of larger societal features but put rather sharp limits on their historical and cross-cultural applicability. The limited nature of such small-scale, social-psychological approaches provides only a partial explanation of social reality which, placed in a broader context of human social relations, reveals merely a small segment of social life that is conditioned by social forces at the larger, structural level.

Notes

1. Erving Goffman, *The Presentation of Self in Everyday Life* (Garden City, N.Y.: Doubleday, 1959), xi.

2. Bernard N. Meltzer, John W. Petras, and Larry T. Reynolds, *Symbolic Interactionism: Genesis, Varieties and Criticism* (London: Routledge & Kegan Paul, 1975), 68.

3. Erving Goffman, *Interaction Ritual: Essays in Face-to-Face Behavior* (Garden City, N.Y.: Doubleday, 1967).

4. See Erving Goffman, *Asylums: Essays on the Social Situation of Mental Patients and Other Inmates* (Garden City, N.Y.: Doubleday, 1961).

5. Ibid.

6. Ibid.

7. Erving Goffman, *Stigma: Notes on the Management of Spoiled Identity* (Englewood Cliffs, N.J.: Prentice-Hall, 1963).

8. Ibid.

9. Ibid.

10. Erving Goffman, *Frame Analysis: An Essay on the Organization of Experience* (Cambridge, Mass.: Harvard University Press, 1974).

11. George Gonos, "'Situation' Versus 'Frame': The 'Interactionist' and the 'Structuralist' Analyses of Everyday Life," *American Sociological Review* 42, no. 6 (December 1977), 855.

12. Goffman, *Frame Analysis*, 1.

13. Ibid., 10.

14. Larry T. Reynolds, *Interactionism: Exposition and Critique*, Third Edition (Dix Hills, N.Y.: General Hall, 1993), 102.

15. See Harold Garfinkel, *Studies in Ethnomethodology* (Englewood Cliffs, N.J.: Prentice-Hall, 1967).

16. Ibid. vii.

17. Meltzer, et. al., *Symbolic Interactionism*, 79.

18. Paul Filmer et al., *New Directions in Sociological Theory* (London: Collier, Macmillan, 1972), 210.

19. Nicolaus Mullins, "Text of a Speech Delivered at the ASA Convention," in Larry T. Reynolds and Janice Reynolds (eds.), *The Sociology of Sociology* (New York: McKay, 1973), 195.

20. William Skidmore, *Theoretical Thinking in Sociology* (Cambridge: Cambridge University Press, 1975), 260.

21. Meltzer et. al., *Symbolic Interactionism*, 79.

22. Randall Collins and Michael Makowski, *The Discovery of Society* (New York: Random House, 1972), 209.

23. Garfinkel, *Studies in Ethnomethodology*, viii.

24. Jack N. Mitchell, *Social Exchange, Dramaturgy, and Ethnomethodology: Toward a Paradigmatic Synthesis* (New York: Elsevier, 1978), 133–134.

25. Garfinkel, *Studies in Ethnomethodology*, 37.

26. Harold Garfinkel, "Perception and the Other." (Unpublished Ph.D. dissertation, Harvard University, 1952).

27. Garfinkel, *Studies in Ethnomethodology*, 65.

28. Ibid., 70.

29. Ibid.

30. Irving Zeitlin, *Rethinking Sociology: A Critique of Contemporary Sociology* (Englewood Cliffs, N.J.: Prentice-Hall, 1973), 187.

31. Ibid.

32. Ibid.

Chapter 17

WILSON AND WILLIE ON RACE, CLASS AND POVERTY

Nearly half a century after the great debate on race and class prompted by W.E.B. Du Bois' and E. Franklin Frazier's contrasting positions on this important question, the publication in 1978 of William Julius Wilson's book *The Declining Significance of Race* set into motion a new round of debate led by Charles Vert Willie on the nature and role of race and class in the United States today.

This chapter examines the central issues raised in this debate by providing a forum for Wilson's and Willie's views on this important and controversial topic.

Wilson on Race and Class

Describing his book *The Declining Significance of Race* as "a study of race and class in the American experience," Wilson points out that its focus is "a rather significant departure" from that of his previous book, *Power, Racism, and Privilege*, in which, he says, he "paid little attention to the role of class in understanding issues of race."[1] "I now feel that many important features of black and white relations in America," he writes, "are not captured when the issue is defined as majority versus minority and that a preoccupation with race and racial conflict obscures fundamental problems that derive from the intersection of class with race."[2] Wilson goes on to state:

> Race relations in America have undergone fundamental changes in recent years, so much so that now the life chances of individual blacks have more to do with their economic class position than with their day-to-day encounters with whites. In earlier years the systematic efforts of whites to suppress blacks were obvious to even the most insensitive observer. Blacks were denied access to valued and scarce resources through various ingenious schemes of racial exploitation, discrimination, and segregation, schemes that were reinforced by elaborate ideologies of racism. But the

> situation has changed. However determinative such practices were for the previous efforts of the black population to achieve racial equality, . . . they do not provide a meaningful explanation of the life chances of black Americans today.[3]

In building his case for a macrosociological, historical analysis of the process of transformation that the African-American community has undergone since the days of slavery, Wilson identifies three distinct stages in the development of race relations in the United States:

> Stage one coincides with antebellum slavery and the early postbellum era and may be designated the period of *plantation economy and racial-caste oppression*. Stage two begins in the last quarter of the nineteenth century and ends at roughly the New Deal era and may be identified as the period of *industrial expansion, class conflict, and racial oppression*. Finally, stage three is associated with the modern, industrial, post-World War II era, which really began to crystallize during the 1960s and 1970s, and may be characterized as the period of *progressive transition from racial inequalities to class inequalities*.[4]

In the antebellum period and in the period from the mid nineteenth to the mid twentieth century, "Racial oppression was deliberate, overt, and is easily documented, ranging from slavery to segregation."[5] However, since the middle of this century, "many of the traditional barriers have crumbled under the weight of the political, social, and economic changes of the civil rights era. A new set of obstacles has emerged from basic structural shifts in the economy."[6] "These obstacles," Wilson explains, "are therefore impersonal but may prove to be even more formidable for certain segments of the black population."[7]

> Specifically, whereas the previous barriers were usually designed to control and restrict the entire black population, the new barriers create hardships essentially for the black underclass; whereas the old barriers were based explicitly on racial motivations derived from intergroup contact, the new barriers have racial significance only in their consequences, not in their origins. In short, whereas the old barriers bore the pervasive features of racial oppression, the new barriers indicate an important and emerging form of class subordination.[8]

Thus, "in the modern industrial period," Wilson writes, "fundamental economic and political changes have made economic class position more important than race"[9] such that "as the influence of race on minority class-stratification decreases, . . . class takes on greater importance in determining the life chances of minority individuals."[10]

> The clear and growing class divisions among blacks today constitute a case in point. It is difficult to speak of a uniform black experience when the black population can be meaningfully stratified into groups whose members range from those who are affluent to those who are impoverished. This of course has not always been the case, because the crystallization of a black class structure is fairly recent.[11]

Wilson argues that the social-economic and political changes in American society during the course of the twentieth century have led to the development of a black class structure that has fostered a growing class division among blacks, such that in "the last quarter of the twentieth century a deepening economic schism seems to be developing in the black community, with the black poor falling further and further behind middle- and upper-income blacks."[12]

> On the one hand, poorly trained and educationally limited blacks of the inner city, including that growing number of black teenagers and young adults, see their job prospects increasingly restricted to the low-wage sector, their unemployment rates soaring to record levels (which remain high despite swings in the business cycle), their labor-force participation rates declining, their movement out of poverty slowing, and their welfare roles increasing. On the other hand, talented and educated blacks are experiencing unprecedented job opportunities that are at least comparable to those of whites with equivalent qualifications. The improved job situation for the more privileged blacks in the corporate and government sectors is related both to the expansion of salaried white-collar positions and to the pressures of state affirmative action programs.[13]

"In view of these developments," Wilson writes, "it would be difficult to argue that the plight of the black underclass is solely a consequence of racial oppression, that is, the explicit and overt efforts of whites to keep blacks subjugated," adding, "in the same way that it would be difficult to explain the rapid economic improvement of the more privileged blacks by arguing that the traditional forms of racial segregation and discrimination still characterize the labor market in American industries."[14] Wilson concludes: "The recent mobility patterns of blacks lend strong support to the view that economic class is clearly more important than race in predetermining job placement and occupational mobility."[15]

Willie on the Persistence of Race and Racism

"Race is one of the most sensitive and sure indicators of the presence or absence of justice in our society," writes Charles Vert Willie.[16] "To repress the guilt of racial discrimination through denial and other means," he adds, "is to permit injustice to fester and erupt from time to time in race riots and other forms of rebellion."[17] Contrary to Wilson's position, with which he disagrees, Willie argues that "race has not declined but continues as a significant variable differentiating blacks from whites at all income levels."[18] He goes on to argue that "racial discrimination is one of the major factors contributing to economic deprivation among blacks."[19]

In contradistinction to Wilson's thesis of the declining significance of race and the increasing importance of class in determining the social position of African-Americans in the United States today, Willie contends that it is race, not class, that plays a central role in determining one's social position: "I would like to introduce a counterhypothesis," Willie writes,

> that the significance of race is increasing and that it is increasing especially for middle-class blacks who, because of school desegregation and affirmative action and other integration programs, are coming into direct contact with whites for the first time for extended interaction.[20]

Against Wilson's emphasis on the physical condition of the black underclass effected by recent changes in the economic structure, which, together with favorable civil rights legislation, has led to improvements in the economic position of the emerging black middle class, Willie focuses on the effects of race and race relations in general and argues that, despite recent economic gains, race continues to play a dominant role in the life experiences of blacks, including especially the black middle class. Stressing the importance of psychological factors, those who suffer most from the effects of these changes, Willie argues, are members of the educated black middle class, not the underclass: "The people who most severely experience the pain of dislocation due to the changing times are the racial minorities who are talented and educated and integrated, not those who are impoverished and isolated."[21]

Responding to Willie's emphasis on the significance of race in black middle-class life resulting from increased black-white contact within this class, Wilson writes:

> I do not disagree with the way in which Willie has proposed his counterhypothesis. Many educated blacks do experience psychological discomfort in new integrated situations. Willie and I could probably draw many personal examples of this. We both are black and we both teach at elite universities. A few years ago almost no blacks were in such positions. But I am sure that neither of us would trade places with a poor black trapped in the ghetto and handcuffed to a menial, dead-end, and poorly paid job. That is the real problem in the black community and no cries about the psychological discomfort of the integrated black elite should distract our attention from the abominable and deleterious physical conditions of the isolated black poor.[22]

"Wilson does not disagree with the counterhypothesis that I offered about the increasing significance of race," Willie writes, "largely because my hypothesis is an attempt to explain the discomfort of some affluent blacks."[23] He adds: "In Wilson's judgement, however, this is not the real problem in the black community. The real problem, as he states it, is 'the abominable and deleterious physical condition of the isolated black poor'."[24]

Poverty and the Plight of the Urban Underclass

In addressing the issues concerning the source(s) of poverty among the black underclass, Willie and Wilson sharply differ on the role of race and class in affecting the "life chances" of segments of the black population leading to the formation of a large and impoverished black underclass. "When I argue that 'the black experience has moved historically from economic racial oppression experienced by virtually all blacks to economic subordination for the black under-class'," Wilson writes, "Willie complains that I cancel 'out racial discrimination as a key cause of poverty among blacks' thereby making it difficult to explain the greater proportion of black families in poverty and the higher unemployment rate for younger blacks."[25] "Once again Willie overlooks or chooses to ignore one of my key arguments," he states, "namely that 'one of the legacies of the racial oppression in previous years is the continued disproportionate black representation in the under-class'."[26] Wilson explains:

> In other words, patterns of racial subjugation in the past created a vast black under-class as the accumulation of disadvantages were passed on from generation to generation and the economic and technological revolution of modern industrial society threatens to insure it a permanent status. Accordingly, even if all racial

> discrimination were eliminated today, the situation of poor blacks will not be substantially improved unless something is done to remove the structural barriers to decent jobs created by changes in our system of production.[27]

Looking at poverty through a class-based approach, Wilson examines the structural impediments that force the underclass into further economic deprivation and argues that

> The current economic problems of the black urban underclass cannot be sufficiently addressed by programs based on the premise that race is the major cause of those problems. They are problems which are more appropriately associated with class subordination—problems which developed from previous experiences with racial oppression, problems which are now compounded by the economic changes of modern industrial society.[28]

Thus, Wilson continues:

> the challenge of economic dislocation in modern industrial society calls for public policy programs to attack inequality on a broad class front, policy programs, in other words, that go beyond the limits of ethnic and racial discrimination by directly confronting the pervasive and destructive features of class subordination.[29]

To Willie, however, the predicament of the urban poor is directly related to race and racism that prolongs their misery. Consequently, Willie characterizes Wilson's conceptualization of the problem of poverty "flawed." But Willie's argument is based more on his disagreement with Wilson concerning the solution(s) to poverty than the analysis itself.

Commenting on policy recommendations that Wilson made in both *The Declining Significance of Race* and his subsequent book *The Truly Disadvantaged*, Willie criticizes Wilson for rejecting population-specific remedies in favor of "economic and social reforms [that] benefit all groups in the United States, not just poor minorities."[30] "Universal approaches may be helpful in preventing poverty but not in correcting the effects of poverty after it has been experienced" writes Willie. "The poor are placed at risk," he says, "when their self-interest and special needs are ignored or subordinated as could happen in a universal approach."[31] Thus, he concludes, Wilson's universal "action-strategy for dealing with poverty and the poor in the United States is wrong"[32]—a conclusion that is debatable due to its own built-in bias in favor of a population-specific strategy based on race which others have rejected as inadequate and ineffective given the current state of race relations in the United States.

Wilson and Willie On Race, Class and Poverty: Toward a Synthesis

Clearly, the Wilson-Willie debate on race and class has generated a number of important questions that have both historical and contemporary significance for understanding race relations in the United States today.

While it is clear that the African-American community has undergone major transformations in its social structure and thus experienced class differentiation based on changes in the labor force structure over the past one hundred years, it is also clear that race continues to play an important role in determining the predicament of African-Americans in the United States today, albeit in different ways and forms within different classes across the racial divide.

It is true, as Wilson contends, that in the economic sector "class has become more important than race in determining black life chances,"[33] but, as Willie insists and Wilson admits, "This is not to deny the importance of racial antagonism in the social-political order, or even suggest that residential, social, and educational discrimination do not form a part of a vicious circle that feeds back to the economic sector. But this circular process is far more relevant for poor blacks than for more privileged blacks"[34] Wilson cautions us.

> In terms of understanding life chances, the economic mobility of privileged blacks has offset the negative consequences of racial discrimination in the social-political order. Indeed, one will only be able to understand the growing class divisions in the black community by recognizing that racial antagonisms in the sociopolitical order have far less effect on black individual or group access to those opportunities and resources that are centrally important for life chances than have racial antagonisms in the economic sector.[35]

Wilson argues that although racial antagonisms and tensions continue to characterize the American social landscape, class divisions among blacks yield differential results in advancing one's class interests. Thus, as the black class structure increasingly resembles the white class structure, middle class blacks will more and more identify their interests with those of middle class whites, as opposed to poor blacks—notwithstanding the fact that they will continue to experience racial tensions and conflict within the middle class itself, for as long as racism in its various forms continues to exist in the United States. The point is that, increasing class differentiation within the black community will make uniform, racially-oriented policies obsolete, as the class nature of such policies will increasingly become transparent. It is in this context that Wilson writes:

> Thus, as the class divisions of the black community grow, it will become increasingly difficult for Willie and other social scientists to mask these differences either by speaking of a uniform or single black experience or by presenting gross statistics that neither reflect significant variations in the resources of various subgroups within the black population nor the differences in the effects of race in the past and the effects of race in the present.[36]

Although Willie opts for a racial explanation when he argues that race is "a significant variable differentiating blacks from whites at all income levels," he nevertheless recognizes the validity of Wilson's class-based argument when he concedes that his "counterhypothesis" on the "increasing significance of race" actually pertains to "middle-class blacks" and is "an attempt to explain the discomfort of some affluent blacks"[37] for it is the "talented and educated" blacks, and "not those who are impoverished and isolated," Willie asserts, who "most severely experience the pain of dislocation due to changing times."[38]

Finally, in line with his emphasis on the declining significance of race in the economic sector, Wilson defends his position by saying:

> It would be shortsighted to view the traditional forms of racial segregation and discrimination as having essentially disappeared in contemporary America; the presence of blacks is still firmly resisted in various institutions and social arrangements. . . . However, in the economic sphere, class has become more important than race in determining black access to privilege and power.[39]

Wilson goes on to state: "when I speak of the declining significance of race, I am neither ignoring the legacy of previous discrimination nor am I arguing that racial discrimination no longer exists."[40] He writes: "My argument that race relations in America have moved from economic racial oppression to a form of class subordination for the less privileged blacks is not meant to suggest that racial conflicts have disappeared or have even been substantially reduced."[41]

Elsewhere, responding to his critics on this issue, Wilson insists: "Nowhere in my book do I argue that race is "irrelevant or insignificant." It is not simply an either-or situation, rather it is a matter of degree. And I strongly emphasize that there is still a strong basis for racial antagonism on the social, community, and political level."[42]

The analysis presented in these pages makes it sufficiently clear that despite differences in their respective positions, both Wilson and Willie provide complimentary perspectives that should be incorporated in some fashion into a synthetic whole, so that we can better conceptualize and address issues that affect different segments of society at various levels. Together, the seemingly opposed viewpoints that appear contradictory at one level are in fact reconcilable at another if one accepts their value in providing explanations for different aspects of the same reality that is, in effect, complementary.

Notes

1. William Julius Wilson, *The Declining Significance of Race*, Second Edition (Chicago: University of Chicago Press, 1980), ix.
2. Ibid.
3. Ibid., 1.
4. Ibid., 2–3 (italics in the original).
5. Ibid., 1.
6. Ibid.
7. Ibid.
8. Ibid., 1–2.
9. Ibid., 23.
10. Ibid., x.
11. Ibid.
12. Ibid., 152.
13. Ibid., 151.
14. Ibid., 151–52.
15. Ibid., 152.
16. Charles Vert Willie, *The Caste and Class Controversy on Race and Poverty*, Second Edition (Dix Hills, N.Y.: General Hall, 1989), 82.
17. Ibid.
18. Ibid., 86.
19. Ibid., 55.
20. Ibid., 20.
21. Ibid., 21.
22. William Julius Wilson, "The Declining Significance of Race: Revisited But Not Revised," in Willie, *The Caste and Class Controversy on Race and Poverty*, 36.
23. Willie, *The Caste and Class Controversy on Race and Poverty*, 39.
24. Ibid.
25. Wilson, "The Declining Significance of Race: Revisited But Not Revised," 31.
26. Ibid., 31.
27. Ibid., 31–32.
28. Wilson, *The Declining Significance of Race*, 165
29. Ibid., 154.
30. William Julius Wilson, *The Truly Disadvantaged* (Chicago: University of Chicago Press, 1987), 155.
31. Willie, *The Caste and Class Controversy on Race and Poverty*, 179.
32. Ibid.
33. Wilson, "The Declining Significance of Race: Revisited But Not Revised," 35.
34. Ibid., 26.
35. Ibid., 26–27.

36. Ibid., 35.
37. Willie, *The Caste and Class Controversy on Race and Poverty*, 39.
38. Ibid., 21.
39. Wilson, *The Declining Significance of Race*, 2.
40. Ibid., 167.
41. Ibid., 23.
42. Wilson, "The Declining Significance of Race: Revisited But Not Revised," 35–36.

Chapter 18

WALLERSTEIN AND WORLD SYSTEMS THEORY

Over the past two decades, since the publication in 1974 of his *The Modern World-System*, Immanuel Wallerstein has played a central role in the formulation of a theory of the global political economy that came to be known as "world systems theory."[1] Providing a comparative-historical approach to the study of societies across national boundaries, Wallerstein has thus introduced a unique perspective to social analysis of states at the global level.

This chapter focuses on the arguments presented by Wallerstein in favor of his world systems perspective, which has become prominent among a group of social scientists who developed an entire school of thought around this theory.

World Systems Theory

With the publication in the mid-1970s of *The Modern World System*, Wallerstein launched a multivolume study of the origins and development of the modern world system in an effort to reexamine the transition from feudalism to capitalism in western Europe and its subsequent development and expansion to the rest of the world.[2] This was followed by Samir Amin's two-volume study of accumulation on a world scale and other studies of the world accumulation process from earlier times to the present.[3] Thus began the formation of an entire school of thought that eventually came to be known as "world systems theory."[4]

Explaining his method in selecting the world system as the unit of analysis, Wallerstein argues that he

> abandoned the idea altogether of taking either the sovereign state or that vaguer concept, the national society, as the unit of analysis. I decided that neither one was a social system and that one could only speak of social change in social systems. The only social system in this scheme was the world system.[5]

"Once we assume that the unit of analysis is such a world-system and not the state or the nation or the people," Wallerstein argues, "then much changes in the outcome of the analysis."

> Most specifically we shift from a concern with the attributive characteristics of states to concern with the relational characteristics of states. We shift from seeing classes (and status groups) as groups within a state to seeing them as groups within a world-economy.[6]

Conceptualizing global power struggles as those in accordance with the requirements of a world system that dominates the global political economy over an entire historical period, the world systems approach attempts to provide tools of analysis to examine contemporary global political developments in the context of the logic of the capitalist world economy that has come to dominate the structure of economic relations on a world scale since the sixteenth century.

The capitalist world economy, argues Wallerstein, brings capitalist and noncapitalist states alike under its sway and determines the nature and course of their development as dictated by the most powerful state in control of the world system in a given historical epoch. But competition and rivalry between the leading states engaged in the struggle for domination of the world system, leaves open the possibility that a dominant state in a particular historical period will be replaced by another:

> While the advantages of the core-states have not ceased to expand throughout the history of the modern world-system, the ability of a particular state to remain in the core sector is not beyond challenge. The hounds are ever to the hares for the position of top dog. Indeed, it may well be that in this kind of system it is not structurally possible to avoid, over a long period of historical time, a circulation of elites in the sense that the particular country that is dominant at a given time tends to be replaced in this role sooner or later by another country.[7]

Moving beyond nation-states and formulating the problem in world-systemic terms, Wallerstein thus provides an alternative explanation of the rise and fall of world systems, which take place in much longer historical periods and constitute the very basis of world historical transformations.

In "The Rise and Future Demise of the World Capitalist System," Wallerstein argues in favor of just such a conceptualization in explaining the origins, development, and future transformation of the capitalist world economy and system.[8] Likewise, situating the problematic in a broader historical context of systemic transformation, Wallerstein elsewhere, in *The Modern World-System* and later in *The Capitalist World-Economy*, attempts to explain the transition from feudalism to capitalism in Western Europe and the subsequent rise and development of the world capitalist system in such world-systemic terms.[9]

The Three-Tiered Model

An essential element in the global analysis of the modern world system is the theory's three-tiered model of "core," "periphery," and "semiperiphery," which divides the world system into three areas or zones defined on the basis of a society's level of development and incorporation into the world system. Moreover, the political-economic content of such incorporation determines whether a given social formation is part of the core, the periphery, or the semiperiphery.[10]

> The organizing principle of this operation is the categorical differentiation of levels of the world-system: core, semiperiphery, and periphery. These zones, distinguished by their different economic functions within the world-economic division of labor . . . structure the assemblage of productive processes that constitute the capitalist world-economy.[11]

"On a world-scale," write Hopkins and Wallerstein, "the processes of the division of labor that define and integrate the world-economy are . . . [those] which we designate as 'core' and 'periphery'."[12] Moreover, "although obviously derivative from the core-periphery conception," they add, "there exists a third category, structurally distinct from core and periphery": "Looking at the world-economy as a whole, . . . [there exists] a basically triadic world-scale division of labor among, now, core states, semiperipheral states, and peripheral areas."[13] Thus:

> The world-economy became basically structured as an increasingly interrelated system of strong "core" and weak "peripheral" states, in which inter-state relations . . . are continually shaped and in turn continually shape the deepening and expanding world-scale division and integration of production.[14]

This brings up the question of "the network(s) of governance or rule in the area in question."[15] "In this respect," write Hopkins and Wallerstein, "incorporation entails the expansion of the world-economy's interstate system":

> Interstate relations and the interstate system overall, in part express and in part circumscribe or structure the world-scale accumulation/production process. In short, the relational networks forming the interstate system are integral to, not outside of, the networks constitutive of the social economy defining the scope and reach of the modern world-system. . . .
>
> Insofar as external areas are incorporated, then—and in the singular development of the modern world-system all have been—the transition period framing incorporation encloses definite directions of change in a once external area's arrangements and processes of rule or governance.[16]

The main feature of the modern world system is, in essence, the transfer of surplus from the periphery to the core of the system, conceptualized in a manner similar to Andre Gunder Frank's "metropolis-satellite" model of domination and "exploitation."[17] The mechanism whereby this transfer takes place is "unequal exchange"[18]—a mechanism made possible by the domination of peripheral states by those in the core:

> Once we get a difference in the strength of the state machineries, we get the operation of "unequal exchange" which is enforced by strong states on weak ones, by core states on peripheral areas. Thus capitalism involves not only appropriation of the surplus value by an owner from a laborer, but an appropriation of surplus of the whole-world-economy by core areas. And this was as true in the stage of agricultural capitalism as it is in the stage of industrial capitalism.[19]

More specifically, Wallerstein argues that without this process of unequal exchange, the capitalist world economy could not exist:

> Such a system [of unequal exchange] is *necessary* for the expansion of a world market if the primary consideration is *profit*. Without *unequal* exchange, it would not be *profitable* to expand the size of the division of labor. And without such expansion, it would not be profitable to maintain a capitalist world-economy, which would then either disintegrate or revert to the form of a redistributive world-empire.[20]

Despite the subordination of peripheral states to those in the core, and the "exploitation" of the former by the latter through surplus extraction, the modern world system allows, under certain conditions and in the context of certain political-economic processes, the transformation of some peripheral states into semiperipheral ones. But such transformation (or mobility) of states along the three-tiered continuum takes place within the context and logic of the system as a whole and as a consequence of the dictates of the dominant world system in a given historical period. Thus the various parts of the system that make up its totality always function within the framework of the relationship of the parts to the whole.

Conclusion

Although world systems theory constitutes a major improvement over mainstream developmentalist theories of the world political economy, it nevertheless suffers from a number of fundamental flaws that must be pointed out. The first, and central, flaw of this theory is the treatment of the world economy and the world system in strictly circulationist terms. Capitalism, defined as a system of accumulation for profit through the market, is conceptualized in the context of exchange relations. Thus, economic relations take place between states within the context of such market exchange. As a result, the question of the mode of production, and its social component relations of production (i.e., class relations), are ignored or eliminated from analysis so that class struggles based on relations of production also disappear from analysis as irrelevant. We are thus left with the generalized abstract notions of "world system" and "world economy" consisting of three zones ("core," "periphery," and "semiperiphery") between which all major global social, political, and economic relations take place. Unfortunately, given its focus on the world system at the global level, the theory fails to provide an explanation of the underlying *class logic* of the world system, its class contradictions and class conflicts.

In the next chapter, we turn to the Marxist class analysis approach provided in the works of Goran Therborn and Albert Szymanski, who introduce into contemporary social theory recent developments in Marxist theory.

Notes

1. Immanuel Wallerstein, *The Modern World-System* (New York: Academic Press, 1974), 53.
2. Ibid.
3. Samir Amin, *Accumulation on a World Scale*, 2 vols. (New York: Monthly Review Press, 1974); Richard Rubinson, ed., *Dynamics of World Development* (London: Sage Publications, 1981). See also the works of Terence Hopkins, Christopher Chase-Dunn, Albert Bergesen, Walter Goldfrank, and Terry Boswell.
4. For an in-depth analysis of the theoretical and methodological premises of world systems theory, see Alvin Y. So, *Social Change and Development: Modernization, Dependenc, and World-System Theories* (Newbury Park, Calif.: Sage Publications, 1990), pt. 3.

5. Wallerstein, *The Modern World-System*, 7.

6. Ibid., xi.

7. Immanuel Wallerstein, "The Rise and Future Demise of the World Capitalist System," *Comparative Studies in Society and History* 16 (September 1974): 350.

8. Ibid.

9. See Wallerstein, *The Modern World-System*; and idem, *The Capitalist World-Economy* (Cambridge, England: Cambridge University Press, 1979).

10. Wallerstein, *The Modern World-System*; and idem, "The Rise and Future Demise of the World Capitalist System."

11. Terence K. Hopkins and Immanuel Wallerstein, *World-Systems Analysis* (Beverly Hills, Calif.: Sage Publications, 1982), 77.

12. Ibid., 45.

13. Ibid., 47.

14. Ibid., 43.

15. Terence K. Hopkins and Immanuel Wallerstein, "Structural Transformations of the World-Economy," in Rubinson, *Dynamics of World Development*, 245.

16. Ibid., 245–46.

17. See Andre Gunder Frank, *Capitalism and Underdevelopment in Latin America* (New York: Monthly Review Press, 1967).

18. This process was first examined at length by Arghiri Emmanuel, *Unequal Exchange: A Study of the Imperialism of Trade* (New York: Monthly Review Press, 1972). Later it was elaborated by Samir Amin, *Unequal Development: An Essay on the Social Formations of Peripheral Capitalism* (New York: Monthly Review Press, 1977).

19. Wallerstein, *The Capitalist World-Economy*, 18–19.

20. Ibid., 71.

Chapter 19

THERBORN AND SZYMANSKI ON CONTEMPORARY MARXIST THEORY

In contrast to the neo-Weberian and world systems theories discussed in the previous two chapters, we now present an overview of recent developments in Marxist theory by focusing on the works of Goran Therborn and Albert Szymanski who provide an alternative, historical-materialist conceptualization of class, state, and society.[1] Advancing a class-based position and incorporating some of the important Marxist theorizing of the 1970s and 1980s into a social theory based on a class-analysis approach informed by the dialectics of the class struggle, Therborn and Szymanski make an important contribution to the resurgence of Marxist theory in recent years.

Historical Materialism and the Base-Superstructure Problematic

The origins of this new wave of Marxist theorizing go back to the late 1970s, when Therborn, Szymanski, and a number of other Marxist intellectuals set forth their theoretical position and thus prepared the stage for the subsequent emergence of works raising questions of paramount importance originally formulated by Marx, Engels, and Lenin.

"This renaissance of Marxist political analysis in the 1980's," writes Therborn, "will appear unexpected":

> The irony is that while many former protagonists and adherents of various "schools" of neo-Marxism are now proclaiming a post-Marxist, beyond-class stance, a new, vigorous self-confident class theory of politics and the state is being launched, impeccably dressed in the best clothes of modern empirical social science, while making no secret of its inspiring commitment to the working-class movement. . . .
>
> There is, then, still a contingent of scholars arguing that states are a function of classes, rather than the other way round.[2]

To his credit, Therborn's contribution to this renaissance has led to a flood of studies in Marxist political economy and class theory of the state and society in the 1980s.

In his book *What Does the Ruling Class Do When It Rules?* Therborn argues in favor of the historical-materialist approach to the study of society, the state, and politics. The aim of such approach, he writes, "is to show that different types of class relations and of class power generate corresponding forms of state organization, and to elucidate the way in which the class character of the state apparatus is determined and revealed."[3]

> According to the axioms of historical materialism, class and state condition each other: where there are no classes, there is no state. In class societies, moreover, social relations are first and foremost class relations. Thus, by definition, every state has a class character, and every class society has a ruling class (or bloc of ruling classes).[4]

Contrary to Hegelian-Marxist and neo-Weberian notions of "state autonomy" and "state-centered" theories that assign primacy to the state and superstructural institutions in society, Therborn reintroduces into the debate the "base-superstructure" problematic, interpreted in a new light—one that avoids economistic conceptualizations of politics on the one hand, while rejecting eclectic "codeterminist" notions of class and state on the other.

Basic to Therborn's analysis of the relationship of the economic base to the political superstructure is the role of the *class struggle* engendered by the dominant mode of production. "In very general terms," writes Therborn,

> the character of state power is defined by the two fundamental processes of determination of the superstructure by the base—processes which in reality are two aspects of the same determination. One of these is the systemic logic of social modes of production, that is to say, the tendencies and contradictions of the specific dynamic of each mode. The other is the struggle of classes, defined by their position in the mode of production. These two forms of determination by the base are logically interrelated in the basic theory of historical materialism.[5]

In this formulation, the state is no longer viewed simply as a passive recipient of directives from the dominant class but is actively involved in the reproduction of the dominant relations of production: "Invariably the state enters into the reproduction of the relations of production by providing the latter with a stabilizing legal framework backed by force."[6] Moreover, the relations of production, Therborn points out, are structured by legal boundaries which define relations between dominant and subordinate classes.[7]

To sum up Therborn's position, "the economic base determines the political superstructure by entering into the reproduction of state power and the state apparatus" and "shapes the character of state power by, among other things, providing the basic parameters of state action."[8] Further, because "exploitative relations of production need a repressive political apparatus as their ultimate guarantee,"[9] the state comes to assume this role to "promote and defend the ruling class and its mode of exploitation or supremacy."[10] Thus, "the ruling class exercises its ruling power over other classes and strata through the state-through holding state power."[11] In order to maintain its legitimacy and secure social order, however, "the state must mediate the exploitation or domination of the ruling class over other classes and strata."[12]

Viewing the base-superstructure problematic in these terms, Therborn bridges the gap between structuralist and instrumentalist formulations of the state and provides a dialectical analysis of the relationship between class and state, thus advancing the debate through a fresh look at historical materialism as the basis for a resurgent Marxist theory of society in this final decade of the twentieth century.

Theory of the State

Albert Szymanski, in his book *The Capitalist State and the Politics of Class*, makes a similar case in favor of the historical-materialist approach to the study of society and the state.[13] Citing the works of Marx, Engels, and Lenin on the state, Szymanski argues that the state plays a central role in society and that "a Marxist political sociology must thus give careful and detailed consideration to the nature of the state."[14]

Examining the nature and role of the state in class society in general and capitalist society in particular, Szymanski writes:

> The state is an instrument by which the exploitation of the economically subordinate class is secured by the economically dominant class that controls the state. . . . The social relationships and the social order that the state guarantees are thus the social relationships of inequality and the order of property and exploitation. . . .
>
> The state in capitalist society is a capitalist state by virtue of its domination by the capitalist class and in that it functions most immediately in the interests of capital.[15]

Moreover, the state must function within the confines of an economic, military, political, and ideological environment structured by capitalist relations of production.[16] This means that the logic of capitalist economic relations, reinforced by capital's ideological hegemony, dictate the policies the state must follow, which are formulated within a very limited range of options allowed by the capitalist mode of production. Thus the state in capitalist society is controlled by the capitalist class through both direct and indirect mechanisms that foster the interests of this class.

Far from providing a simple instrumentalist view of the state, Szymanski reveals the full range and complexity of the state's actions in response to the ensuing class struggles in society: "Political outcomes are the result of the relative size, social location, consciousness, degree of organization, and strategies followed by classes and segments of classes in their ongoing struggles."[17] He goes on to point out that "no one class or segment of a class is ever able totally to control all aspects of society."[18] Moreover, while the state "is normally under the domination of the class that owns and controls the means of production,"

> the ruling class must take into account both the demands and likely responses of other classes when it makes state policy. If it does not it may suffer very serious consequences, including social revolution.[19]

"The degree of relative autonomy of the state bureaucracy from direct capitalist-class domination," writes Szymanski, "can either decrease *or* increase drastically during an economic and social crisis":

> A state that is too directly dominated by the majority bloc of the capitalist class may be unable to handle such a crisis, because the narrow-minded self-interest of this bloc prevents the state it dominates from adopting the policies necessary to save and advance the system. Domination of the state by these groups also tends to discredit the state, which because of such control is obviously not alleviating an economic crisis. The legitimating function of the state thus comes into increasing conflict with direct capitalist-class control.[20]

Providing an empirical path out of the structuralist-instrumentalist problematic, Szymanski argues that some states are dominated principally by direct mechanisms, while others are dominated by indirect mechanisms, and still others are dominated by *both*.

Commenting on the question of relative autonomy, David Gold, Clarence Y.H. Lo, and Erik Olin Wright make a similar argument when they point out that such autonomy "is not an invariant feature of the capitalist state":

> Particular capitalist states will be more or less autonomous depending upon the degree of internal divisiveness, the contradictions within the various classes and fractions which constitute the power bloc, and upon the intensity of class struggle between the working class and the capitalist class as a whole.[21]

In Europe, for example, given the differential political development of some European formations (e.g., France, Italy, Spain, and Greece) where strong socialist and communist parties and movements have developed and flourished, it has been difficult for capital to maintain direct, exclusive control of the state apparatus and yield results always in line with its interests. In these formations, the state has been shaped not only by the various fractions of the capitalist class but also by the representatives of rival opposition forces, including the socialists and the communists, contending for state power. This situation has invariably been effected through the presence of opposition forces within the very organs and institutions of the state. As the power and influence of these parties have increased disproportionately vis-à-vis that of the capitalists, a resurgence of the class struggle and struggles for state power have occurred—sometimes leading to the possession of political power by socialist and communist forces in key state institutions, such as the parliament or the presidency and cabinet posts within the executive branch, as in Spain, France, Italy, and Greece, as well as elsewhere in Europe at various levels of government in local and national politics.

In contrast, in the United States, except possibly during crisis periods (such as the Great Depression of the 1930s) when there has been a resurgence of class politics, the state has been completely dominated and controlled by the capitalist class, now especially by its monopoly fraction. This, coupled with the relative weakness of the U.S. labor movement, has led capital to directly control the U.S. state. Thus, it is not surprising that an instrumentalist view of the state has so readily become the predominant mode of state theorizing among Marxists in the United States.

The greater strength and militancy of the organized working-class movement and effective opposition of independent workers' parties and organizations in Europe, on the other hand, has effected the distribution of power among a multitude of political parties and coalition governments. Thus, it is likewise not surprising that a structuralist theory of the state would emerge to provide an alternative explanation of the nature and dynamics of politics and the state in Europe during this same period.

Thus the role of direct and indirect mechanisms of capitalist-class rule, as well as the degree of autonomy of the state, has varied considerably among formations dominated by the capitalist mode of production. These variations point to the need for a concrete analysis of states across national boundaries and over extended historical periods.

Conclusion

The centerpiece of the resurgent Marxist theory of society and the state has been its focus on the nature of class relations, class struggles, and the class character of the state. Situated within the framework of the base-superstructure problematic of historical materialism, Marxist theory has taken center stage in social theorizing and is now experiencing a resurgence among a growing contingent of critical social theorists in addressing the pressing problems of contemporary capitalist society. Therborn and Szymanski have been among the pioneers of this resurgence of critical thinking in sociology and the social sciences during the 1980s; others, promoting their views among a new generation of critical social theorists, are now playing a central role in the development of this important trend in social theory in the decade of the 1990s and into the next century.

Notes

1. For Therborn's most important works, see Goran Therborn, *Science, Class and Society* (London: New Left Books, 1976), esp. 317–429; idem, *What Does the Ruling Class Do When It Rules?* (London: New Left Books, 1978); and idem, *The Ideology of Power and the Power of Ideology* (London: New Left Books, 1980). For some of Szymanski's most important works, see Albert Szymanski, *The Capitalist State and the Politics of Class* (Cambridge, Mass.: Winthrop, 1978); idem, *The Logic of Imperialism* (New York: Praeger, 1981); and idem, *Class Structure: A Critical Perspective* (New York: Praeger, 1983).

2. Goran Therborn, "Neo-Marxist, Pluralist, Corporatist, Statist Theories and the Welfare State," in *The State in Global Perspective*, ed. A. Kazancigil (Aldershot, England: and UNESCO, 1986), 205–6.

3. Therborn, *What Does the Ruling Class Do?* 35.

4. Ibid., 132.

5. Ibid., 162.

6. Ibid., 165.

7. Ibid.

8. Ibid., 169.

9. Therborn, *Science, Class and Society*, 400–1.

10. Therborn, *What Does the Ruling Class Do?*, 181.

12. Ibid.

13. Szymanski, *The Capitalist State and the Politics of Class.*

14. Ibid., 20–21.

15. Ibid., 21, 25.

16. Ibid., 24.

17. Ibid., 27.

18. Ibid.

19. Ibid.

20. Ibid., 273.

21. David Gold, Clarence Y.H. Lo, and Erik Olin Wright, "Some Recent Developments in Marxist Theories of the Capitalist State," *Monthly Review* 27, nos. 5–6 (October and November, 1975): 38.

Chapter 20

HARVEY AND CALLINICOS ON POSTMODERNISM AND ITS CRITIQUE

During the past two decades contemporary social theory has undergone some important changes resulting from the emergence of various forms of critical discourse. Among these, one finds "postmodernist theory." Those opting for this alternative to both mainstream and Marxist approaches to the study of modern society, have introduced into their analysis the theory and practice of "postmodernity," an era that allegedly characterizes contemporary, "postindustrial" society.

This chapter presents a critical analysis of postmodernism and postmodernist theory through a piercing critique that David Harvey and Alex Callinicos have provided of this latest fad in contemporary social theory. Harvey and Callinicos confront the myths surrounding this most recent theoretical expression of a group of disaffected intellectuals searching for answers in a period of societal crisis and decline in the late twentieth century. In doing so, they reaffirm the validity of historical materialism as a viable theoretical alternative that has stood the test of time.

Postmodernism

What is "postmodernism" and what does it represent? What are its origins and fault-lines that define the limits of what it can offer to advance contemporary social theory? And, why has it become so popular among a group of intellectuals at a particular historical conjuncture characterized by epochal decline reflected in the pessimism of our time? Harvey and Callinicos take up these and other questions surrounding the controversy over postmodernist theory in their recent books *The Condition of Postmodernity* and *Against Postmodernism*, respectively, and provide a critical analysis of its underlying assumptions and arguments through a theoretical discourse that is at once complex and comprehensible.[1]

"Does postmodernism . . . represent a radical break with modernism, or is it simply a revolt within modernism against a certain form of 'high modernism'?" asks Harvey.

> Is postmodernism a style . . . or should we view it strictly as a periodizing concept . . . ? Does it have a revolutionary potential by virtue of its opposition to all forms of meta-narratives (including Marxism, Freudianism, and all forms of Enlightenment reason) and its close attention to 'other worlds' and to 'other voices' that have for too long been silenced (women, gays, blacks, colonized peoples with their own histories)? Or is it simply commercialization and domestication of modernism, and a reduction of the latter's already tarnished aspirations to a *laissez-faire*, 'anything goes' market eclecticism? Does it, therefore, undermine or integrate with neo-conservative politics? And do we attach its rise to some radical restructuring of capitalism, the emergence of some 'postindustrial' society, view it, even, as the 'art of an inflationary era' or as the 'cultural logic of late capitalism' (as Newman and Jameson have proposed)?[2]

"Postmodernism," Callinicos points out, "represents the convergence of three distinct cultural trends. . . . Postmodern art, poststructuralist philosophy, and the theory of postindustrial society":

> The first involved certain changes in the arts over the previous couple of decades—in particular, the reaction against the International Style in architecture associated with such names as Robert Venturi and James Sterling which first brought the term 'Post-modern' into popular usage. . . . Secondly, however, a certain current in philosophy was thought to be giving conceptual expression to the themes explored by contemporary artists. This was a group of French theorists who came in the 1970s to be known in the English-speaking world by the shared label of 'poststructuralism'—in particular, Gilles Deleuze, Jacques Derrida and Michel Foucault. . . . But, thirdly, art and philosophy seemed to reflect (somewhat at odds with poststructuralism's anti-realism) changes in the social world. A version of the transformations supposedly undergone by Western societies in the past quarter century was provided by the theory of postindustrial society developed by sociologists such as Daniel Bell and Alain Touraine.[3]

While representing a qualitatively new development in society that appears to be distinct from that characteristic of modernity, postmodernism is nevertheless viewed by its adherents as an outgrowth of modernist thought and practice transformed into new forms of expression that goes beyond the original parameters of modernity itself. In fact, as the attached table of dichotomies of modernism and postmodernism illustrate, the postmodernist project turns out to be quite the opposite of the modernist mode—a classic dialectical resolution of its original contradictions. Postmodernity, then, arises out of its modern origins, and in doing so it becomes something quite different. But such a view is not entirely consistent with all its proponents, some of whom differ on the nature, magnitude, and historic context of postmodernism's decisive break with modernity.

Selected Dichotomies of Modernism and Postmodernism

Modernism	Postmodernism
romanticism/Symbolism	paraphysics/Dadaism
form (conjunctive, closed)	antiform (disjunctive, open)
design	chance
hierarchy	anarchy
art object/finished work	process/performance/happening
totalization/synthesis	deconstruction/antithesis
semantics	rhetoric
paradigm	syntagm
root/depth	rhizome/surface
narrative/grande histoire	anti-narrative/petit histoire
metaphysics	irony
determinacy	indeterminacy

Source: Adopted from I. Hassan, "The Culture of Postmodernism," *Theory, Culture, and Society*, Vol. 2, No. 3 (1985), 123–124.

"For postmodernists," writes Callinicos, "the decisive break is usually with the Enlightenment, with which . . . Modernism tends to be identified."[4] In the economic sphere, however, this break is marked with the shift from industrial production to services and information technology, hence from the industrial to the "postindustrial" stage. An argument based largely on Daniel Bell's conception of "post-industrial society," this aspect of post-modernist thought identifies a manifestation of late capitalist development as a qualitatively distinct stage of human development to warrant it the "post-industrial" or "postmodernist" label. "What runs through all the various—mutually and often internally inconsistent—accounts of Postmodernism," writes Callinicos, "is the idea that recent aesthetic changes (however characterized) are symptomatic of a broader, radical novelty, a sea-change in Western civilization."[5]

"This sea-change," Harvey points out, "is bound up with the emergence of new dominant ways in which we experience space and time."[6] He writes:

> While simultaneity in the shifting dimensions of time and space is no proof of necessary or casual connection, strong a priori grounds can be adduced for the proposition that there is some kind of necessary relation between the rise of postmodernist cultural forms, the emergence of more flexible modes of capital accumulation, and a new round of 'time-space compression' in the organization of capitalism.[7]

"A little before the postmodern boom got into full swing," Callinicos reminds us, "Daniel Bell noted the widespread 'sense of an ending' among the Western intelligentsia 'symbolized . . . in the widespread use of the word post . . . to define, as a combined form, the age into which we are moving'."[8] "Bell illustrated this proliferation of 'posts-'," Callinicos notes, "by listing the following examples:"

> post-capitalist, post-bourgeois, post-modern, post-civilized, post-collectivist, post-Puritan, post-Protestant, post-Christian, post-literature, post-traditional, post-historical, post-market society, post-organization society, post-economic, post-scarcity, post-welfare, post-liberal, post-industrial . . .[9]

Although, as Harvey points out, "traditional neoconservatives, such as Daniel Bell, fear rather than welcome" any affinity to postmodernist thought, as "Bell plainly regrets the collapse of solid bourgeois values, the erosion of the work ethic in the working class, and sees contemporary trends less as a turn towards a vibrant postmodernist future and more as an exhaustion of modernism,"[10] the postmodernists have nevertheless been influenced just as much by Bell's postindustrialism as Jean-Francois Lyotard's leftwing anti-institutionalism.

Counterposed to Bell's bourgeois critique of "postindustrial" developments that have engendered "the cultural contradictions of capitalism" which Bell despises, Lyotard provides an alternative view of such developments that welcomes an era when new forms of cultural practice are "supplanting permanent institutions in the professional, emotional, sexual, cultural, family, and international domains, as well as in political affairs."[11]

Despite the divergent political views embodied in the two politically contradictory positions, it is the convergence of these two positions on the nature of the postindustrial, postmodern condition that defines for the postmodernists the cultural parameters of postmodernism in the late twentieth century.

Critique of Postmodernism

In providing a critique of postmodernism and postmodernist thought, Callinicos and Harvey raise a number of important issues that are central to an understanding of what postmodernism is and what the postmodernist intellectuals propose in their anti-modernist project.

In seeing themselves as part of "a wilful and rather chaotic movement to overcome all the supposed ills of modernism," Harvey argues, "postmodernists exaggerate when they depict the modern as grossly as they do."[12] He writes:

> postmodernism, with its emphasis upon the ephemerality of *jouissance*, its insistence upon the impenetrability of the other, its concentration on the text rather than the work, its penchant for deconstruction bordering on nihilism, its preference for aesthetics over ethics, takes matters too far. It takes them beyond the point where any coherent politics are left, while that wing of it that seeks a shameless accommodation with the market puts it firmly in the tracks of an entrepreneurial culture that is the hallmark of reactionary neoconservativism.[13]

"Postmodernist philosophers tell us," Harvey continues, "not only to accept but even to revel in the fragmentations and the cacophony of voices through which the dilemmas of the modern world are understood."[14] He says:

> Obsessed with deconstructing and delegitimating every form of argument they encounter, they can end only in condemning their own validity claims to the point where nothing remains of any basis for reasoned action. Postmodernism has us accepting the reifications and partitionings, actually celebrating the activity of masking and cover-up, all the fetishisms of locality, place, or social grouping, while denying that kind of meta-theory which can grasp the political-economic processes (money flows, international divisions of labor, financial markets, and the like) that are becoming ever more universalizing in their depth, intensity, reach and power over daily life.[15]

"Worst of all," Harvey concludes, "while it opens up a radical prospect by acknowledging the authenticity of other voices,"

> postmodernist thinking immediately shuts off those other voices from access to more universal sources of power by ghettoizing them within an opaque otherness, the specificity of this or that language game. It thereby disempowers those voices (of women, ethnic and racial minorities, colonized peoples, the unemployed, youth, etc.) in a world of lop-sided power relations.[16]

Lending support to Harvey's contentions, Callinicos argues that while postmodernists' rejection of anything associated with the modernist past and their self-defined affinity with the powerless appears to be revolutionary, postmodernism in reality turns its back on social revolution, providing support instead to those longing for individual expression that is anti-institutional and self-centered—a postmodern version of the anarchy of thought that supports an intellectual discourse in a society that lacks an aesthetic identity and logic. The chaos that emerges from all this is what identifies the nature and purpose of eclecticism of the mind, prompting Frank Kermode to call postmodernism "another of those period descriptions that help you to take a view of the past suitable to whatever it is you want to do."[17]

"Postmodernity," Callinicos points out, "is merely a theoretical construct, of interest primarily as a symptom of the current mood of the Western intelligentsia."[18] Its roots lie in the pessimism prevalent in a period of decline and decay in centers of world capitalism in the closing decades of the twentieth century—a condition reinforced by the perceived failure of socialist revolution in the advanced capitalist countries.

> The discourse of postmodernism is best seen as the product of a socially mobile intelligentsia in a climate dominated by the retreat of the Western labor movement and the 'overconsumptionist' dynamic of capitalism in the Reagan-Thatcher era. From this perspective the term 'postmodern' would seem to be a floating signifier by means of which this intelligentsia has sought to articulate its political disillusionment and its aspiration to a consumption-oriented lifestyle. The difficulties involved in identifying a referent for this term are therefore beside the point, since talk about postmodernism turns out to be less about the world than the expression of a particular generation's sense of an ending.[19]

"The political odyssey of the 1968 generation," Callinicos writes, "is, in my view, crucial to the widespread acceptance of the idea of a postmodern epoch in the 1980s."

> This was the decade when those radicalized in the 1960s and early 1970s began to enter middle age. Usually they did so with all hope of socialist revolution gone—indeed, often having ceased to believe in the desirability of any such revolution. Most of them had by then come to occupy some sort of professional, managerial or administrative position, to have become members of the new middle class, at a time when the overconsumptionist dynamic of

> Western capitalism offered this class rising living standards (a benefit often denied the rest of the workforce: hourly real wages in the U.S. fell by 8.7 per cent between 1973 and 1986). This conjuncture—the prosperity of the Western new middle class combined with the political disillusionment of many of its most articulate members—provides the context to the proliferating talk of postmodernism.[20]

Postmodernity, then, is a reaction to the reality of late twentieth century capitalism as it is translated into a mythical future to cope with the material contradictions of modernity that the Western intelligentsia now confronts. And in this way, the postmodernist discourse claims to transcend the boundaries of what has until now been real and venture into that what is claimed to be in the making in the postmodernist journey that we are purported to have begun and are destined to travel.

Critics of postmodernism, however, disagree with such claims of the occurrence of a great socio-cultural transformation. For Frederic Jameson, for example, postmodernism and all that it embodies is a product of the cultural logic of late capitalism, and the accompanying changes that it has effected in society do not constitute a social or cultural transformation of epochal proportions.[21] "If there has been some kind of transformation in the political economy of late twentieth-century capitalism," writes David Harvey, "then it behooves us to establish how deep and fundamental the change might be."[22]

> Signs and tokens of radical changes in labor processes, in consumer habits, in geographical and geopolitical configurations, in state powers and practices, and the like, abound. Yet we still live, in the West, in a society where production for profit remains the basic organizing principle of economic life. We need some way, therefore, to represent all the shifting and churning that has gone on since the first major post-war recession of 1973, which does not lose sight of the fact that the basic rules of a capitalist mode of production continue to operate as invariant shaping forces in historical-geographical development.[23]

Thus, "there is much more continuity than difference between the broad history of modernism and the movement called postmodernism" Harvey concludes:

> It seems more sensible to me to see the latter as a particular kind of crisis within the former, one that emphasizes the fragmentary, the

> ephemeral, and the chaotic side of Baudelaire's formulation (that side which Marx so admirably dissects as integral to the capitalist mode of production) while expressing a deep skepticism as to any particular prescriptions as to how the eternal and immutable should be conceived of, represented, or expressed.[24]

Hence:

> Whether or not the new systems of production and marketing, characterized by more flexible labor processes and markets, of geographical mobility and rapid shifts in consumption practices, warrant the title of a new regime of accumulation, and whether the revival of entrepreneurialism and of neoconservatism, coupled with the cultural turn to postmodernism, warrant the title of a new mode of regulation, is by no means clear. There is always a danger of confusing the transitory and the ephemeral with more fundamental transformations in political-economic life.[25]

Callinicos likewise criticizes postmodernist claims of a qualitative social transformation by arguing that the sociocultural changes the postmodernists allude to do not represent the arrival of a "new age," but that the changes that we are now witnessing are part of the process of modern capitalist development over the past two centuries. He writes:

> I do not believe that we live in 'New Times', in a 'postindustrial and postmodern age' fundamentally different from the capitalist mode of production globally dominant for the past two centuries. I deny the main theses of poststructuralism, which seem to me in substance false. I doubt very much that Postmodern art represents a qualitative break from the Modernism of the early twentieth century. Moreover, much of what is written in support of the idea that we live in a postmodern epoch seems to me of small calibre intellectually, usually superficial, often ignorant, sometimes incoherent.[26]

"Whatever else we do with the concept," concludes Harvey, "we should not read postmodernism as some autonomous artistic current. Its rootedness in daily life is one of its most patently transparent features."[27]

This, in essence, is the critique of postmodernism and postmodernist thought which, as both Callinicos and Harvey have shown, is part of a larger critique of the most recent contradictions of capitalism in the late twentieth century.

Return to Historical Materialism?

Callinicos and Harvey counter the postmodernist myth of a postindustrial society by stressing the necessity of returning to an analysis of society and social relations provided by historical materialism.

Highlighting the superiority of historical materialism over postmodernist modes of thought, "Marx's greater optimism about the scope for human emancipation," writes Callinicos, "rested on his deeper historical understanding of the transitory nature of the social structures that have shaped our existence for the past few millennia."[28] In this context, Callinicos states: "perhaps we should think of modernity as the kind of civilization formed by the development and global dominance of the capitalist mode of production."[29] And, as an extension, one could view postmodernity as a continuation of the capitalist mode of production and its contradictions in the late twentieth century.

Historical materialism, Harvey reminds us, "is an open-ended and dialectical mode of enquiry rather than a closed and fixed body of understandings. Meta-theory is not a statement of total truth but an attempt to come to terms with the historical and geographical truths that characterize capitalism both in general as well as in its present phase."[30] Clearly, such a reasoning would force us to confront the dialectical logic of capitalism's inherent class contradictions which, according to this logic, could be resolved only by a working-class revolution.

Callinicos' and Harvey's perceptive analysis of postmodernism and postmodernist thought shows the invaluable contribution of historical materialism as the only viable approach that helps us understand the nature and dynamics of the modern world and its postmodern variants through an analysis of society that probes deeply into the human condition, without resorting to the intellectual detours and confusion invoked by contemporary postmodernist discourse that has become fashionable among the intellectual elite.

Notes

1. See David Harvey, *The Condition of Postmodernity* (Cambridge, Mass.: Blackwell, 1990) and Alex Callinicos, *Against Postmodernism* (New York: St. Martin's Press, 1989).
2. Harvey, *The Condition of Postmodernity*, 42.
3. Callinicos, *Against Postmodernism*, 2–3.
4. Ibid., 25.
5. Ibid.
6. Harvey, *The Condition of Postmodernity*, vii.
7. Ibid.
8. Callinicos, *Against Postmodernism*, 25.
9. Ibid.

10. Harvey, *The Condition of Postmodernity*, 113.

11. Jean-Francois Lyotard, *The Postmodern Condition* (Minneapolis: University of Minnesota Press, 1984).

12. Harvey, *The Condition of Postmodernity*, 115.

13. Ibid., 116.

14. Ibid.

15. Ibid., 116–117.

16. Ibid., 117.

17. Frank Kermode, *History and Value* (Oxford, 1988), 132.

18. Callinicos, *Against Postmodernism*, 9.

19. Alex Callinicos, "Reactionary Postmodernism?" in R. Boyne and A. Rattansi (ed.), *Postmodernism and Social Theory*.

20. Callinicos, *Against Postmodernism*, 168.

21. Frederic Jameson, "Postmodernism, or the Cultural Logic of Late Capitalism,' *New Left Review* 146 (1984), 53–92.

22. Harvey, *The Condition of Postmodernity*, 121.

23. Ibid.

24. Ibid., 116.

25. Ibid., 124.

26. Callinicos, *Against Postmodernism*, 4–5.

27. Harvey, *The Condition of Postmodernity*, 63.

28. Callinicos, *Against Postmodernism*, 172–173.

29. Ibid., 36.

30. Harvey, *The Condition of Postmodernity*, 355.

CONCLUSION

The varieties of social theory discussed in this brief introductory book represent a sampling of the rich heritage of diverse theoretical perspectives in sociology and related disciplines in the social sciences. They provide us with a multitude of explanations on different aspects of social life, encompassing the economy, society, and polity. While the traditions of classical social theory inform contemporary theorizing in sociology, thus cultivating the contributions of the great social thinkers of the past century, modern social theorists of the twentieth century have made their own unique contribution to the study of society, providing answers to the burning questions of our time from a variety of diverse theoretical perspectives.

Although Durkheim, Weber, and Marx are viewed as classical reference points in sociological theory, representing the three alternative approaches—organic, individualistic, and organizational—that have come to define the boundaries of the rival schools of thought in contemporary sociology, other, though somewhat less influential, theorists of the late nineteenth and early twentieth centuries have also made important contributions to classical and contemporary social theory, so that theorists as diverse as Pareto, Freud, Gramsci, Du Bois, Parsons, Merton, Mills, Poulantzas, Wallerstein, and Therborn have made their mark within the broader parameters of modern social theory.

This accumulated source of knowledge over the past century, with parallel developments in a variety of competing paradigms in social theory, has led to a combination of diverse approaches yielding numerous new theoretical syntheses (e.g., neo-Weberian, neo-Marxist, and neo-Freudian), as well as the establishment of entire schools of thought cultivated by such intellectual cross-fertilization (e.g., the Frankfurt School of critical theory, structural functionalism, symbolic interactionism, and varieties of structuralist theorizing).

More recently, there has emerged "postmodernist" modes of thought, which attempt to explain the contours of the "postcapitalist" social order. Theorists opting for this most recent attempt at critical theorizing, which rejects both mainstream and Marxist analyses of contemporary society, have introduced into their cultural analysis the theory and praxis of "postmodernity," an era that allegedly characterizes contemporary, "postindustrial" society. These self-defined analysts of the "postmodern age," however, have come under strong criticism for promoting yet another fad in social theory whose roots lie in the pessimism prevalent in a period of decline and decay in centers of world capitalism in the closing decades of the twentieth century.

The theoretical defects in postmodernist discourse on the nature and sources of this transformation notwithstanding, the contemporary crisis of world capitalism has generated intense discussion and debate between and within the leading schools of thought and engendered the emergence of a variety of alternative theoretical positions. Clearly, social theory cannot be divorced from the prevailing material conditions in society. And these conditions often give rise to a variety of intellectual responses that evolve into various theoretical positions that, in turn, attempt to address the social transformations we are experiencing today. Thus the dialectical interaction between theory and practice over time comes to inform our conception of the social world and further contributes to a better understanding of the prevailing conditions in society.

We have in this book attempted to provide a glimpse of classical and contemporary attempts by a variety of social theorists to tackle the central questions of our time—questions that define the human condition in all its complexities. Theorists with differing views on human nature, the nature of society, the role of the individual and social institutions, as well as other dimensions of social, economic, and political life that define the totality of social relations and the social order, have made eloquent arguments in favor of their positions on these questions, which we have critically examined in this book.

We have shown that much of the theoretical discourse among the classical social theorists of the late nineteenth and early twentieth centuries has been in reaction to the arguments advanced by Marx on a variety of questions concerning society. Durkheim, Weber, Pareto, Mosca, Mead, Freud, Gramsci, Lenin, and a host of other social theorists of this period developed their theories as an extension of or in direct opposition to the ideas expounded by Marx, who is viewed by many as the greatest social theorist of the nineteenth century. Through a brilliant transformation of the Hegelian dialectic and a dynamic reconceptualization of classical materialism, Marx went on to develop a materialist conception of history and explained it dialectically. Going a step further, he insisted that "the philosophers have only *interpreted* the world, in various ways; the point, however, is to *change* it." Thus, dialectical and historical materialism, committed to a scientific analysis of society and its transformation, became the hallmark of the Marxist approach that has set the broader parameters of discussion and debate in social theory over the past century.

The ongoing controversies in sociology and the other social sciences on the nature of contemporary society, economy, and polity are an extension of these earlier debates and have yielded a variety of diverse theoretical approaches, including Parsonian, Millsian, Althusserian, neo-Weberian, neo-Marxist, and "postmodernist" formulations. Herein lies the importance of classical and contemporary social theory, which has contributed in different ways to the totality of the knowledge we have come to obtain about society—a knowledge that is a direct product of the constant subjection of theory to the test of social reality.

The constant interaction of this continuously expanding theoretical knowledge with the changing conditions of social reality (i.e., between theory and practice) in the end informs our conception of different aspects of life in contemporary society—a process that highlights the importance of social theory as a tool for analysis to sort out the complex phenomena that define the nature and scope of human relations in society. For this reason, sociologists place great value on the pivotal role of social theory in the study of society.

BIBLIOGRAPHY

Althusser, Louis. 1971. "Ideology and Ideological State Apparatuses." In L. Althusser, *Lenin and Philosophy and Other Essays*. London: New Left Books.

——. 1976. *Essays in Self-Criticism*. London: New Left Books.

Althusser, Louis, and Etienne Balibar. 1968. *Reading Capital*. London: New Left Books.

Aptheker, Herbert. 1960. *The World of C. Wright Mills*. New York: Marzani and Munsell.

——. 1973. *Annotated Bibliography of the Published Writings of W.E.B. Du Bois*. Millwood, N.Y.: Kraus-Thomson.

——. 1990. "W.E.B. Du Bois: Struggle Not Despair." *Clinical Sociology Review* 8.

Bellah, Robert N. 1959. "Durkheim and History." *American Sociological Review* 24, no. 4 (August).

Berberoglu, Berch. 1990. *Political Sociology*. Dix Hills, N.Y.: General Hall.

——. 1991. *Critical Perspectives in Sociology*. Dubuque, Iowa: Kendall/Hunt.

——. 1992. *The Legacy of Empire: Economic Decline and Class Polarization in the United States*. New York: Praeger.

——. 1992. *The Political Economy of Development*. Albany, N.Y.: SUNY Press.

——. 1993. *The Labor Process and Control of Labor: The Changing Nature of Work Relations in the Late 20th Century*. New York: Praeger.

——. 1994. *Class Structure and Social Transformation*. New York: Praeger.

——. 1995. *The National Question: Nationalism, Ethnic Conflict, and Self-Determination in the 20th Century*. Philadelphia: Temple University Press.

Birnbaum, Norman. 1971. *Toward a Critical Sociology*. New York: Oxford University Press.

Blackwell, James E., and Morris Janowitz, eds. 1974. *Black Sociologists: Historical and Contemporary Perspectives*. Chicago: University of Chicago Press.

Block, Fred. 1977. "The Ruling Class Does Not Rule: Notes on the Marxist Theory of the State." *Socialist Review*, no. 33 (May–June).

——. 1977. "Marxist Theories of the State in World System Analysis." Paper presented at the First Annual Political Economy of the World System Conference, American University, Washington, D.C.

——. 1978. "Class Consciousness and Capitalist Rationalization: A Reply to Critics." *Socialist Review*, nos. 40–41 (July–October).

——. 1987. *Revising State Theory*. Philadelphia: Temple University Press.

Bottomore, T.B. 1966. *Elites and Society*. Baltimore: Penguin.

Bottomore, Tom, and Robert J. Brym, eds. 1989. *The Capitalist Class: An International Study*. New York: New York University Press.

Callinicos, Alex. 1989. *Against Postmodernism: A Marxist Critique*. New York: St. Martin's Press.

Calvert, Peter. 1982. *The Concept of Class*. New York: St. Martin's Press.

Carnoy, Martin. 1984. *The State and Political Theory*. Princeton: Princeton University Press.

Clarke, S. 1977. "Marxism, Sociology and Poulantzas's Theory of the State." *Capital and Class* 2.

Collins, Randall and Michael Makowsky. 1972. *The Discovery of Society*. New York: Random House.

Comte, Auguste. 1893. *The Positive Philosophy*. London: Kegan Paul.

Cooley, Charles Horton. 1902. *Human Nature and Social Order.* New York: Scribner's.
——. 1909. *Social Organization.* New York: Scribner's.
——. 1918. *Social Process.* New York: Scribner's.
Cooper, John Milton, Jr. 1986. "Foreword." Manning Marable, *W.E.B. Du Bois: Black Radical Democrat.* Boston: Twayne.
Crompton, Rosemary, and Jon Gubbay. 1978. *Economy and Class Structure.* New York: St. Martin's Press.
Dahrendorf, Ralph. 1959. *Class and Class Conflict in Industrial Society.* Stanford: Stanford University Press.
Davis, Kingsley, and Wilbert E. Moore, 1945. "Some Principles of Stratification." *American Sociological Review* 10, no. 2 (April).
Dazhina, I.M., et al., eds. 1984. *Alexandra Kollontai: Selected Articles and Speeches.* New York: International Publishers.
Deegan, Mary Jo, ed. 1991. *Women in Sociology.* Westport, Conn.: Greenwood Press.
Domhoff, G. William. 1967. *Who Rules America?* Englewood Cliffs, N.J.: Prentice Hall.
——. 1971. *The Higher Circles: The Governing Class in America.* New York: Vintage.
——. 1978. *The Powers That Be: Processes of Ruling Class Domination in America.* New York: Vintage.
——. 1983. *Who Rules America Now? A View for the '80s.* New York: Simon & Schuster.
——. 1990. *The Power Elite and the State.* New York: Aldine de Gruyter.
Domhoff, G. William, and Hoyt B. Ballard, eds. 1968. *C. Wright Mills and the Power Elite.* Boston: Beacon Press.
Draper, Hal. 1977. *Karl Marx's Theory of Revolution: State and Bureaucracy.* Pts. 1 and 2. New York: Monthly Review Press.
Du Bois, W.E.B. 1953. "Negroes and the Crisis of Capitalism in the United States." *Monthly Review* 4 (April).
——. 1970. "The Social Effects of Emancipation" and "The Class Struggle." in *W.E.B. Du Bois: A Reader*, ed. Meyer Weinberg. New York: Harper & Row.
——. 1975. "The White Masters of the World." In *The Writings of W.E.B. Du Bois*, ed. Virginia Hamilton. New York: Crowell.
Durkheim, Emile. 1951. *Suicide: A Study in Sociology.* New York: Free Press.
——. 1957. *The Elementary Forms of Religious Life.* London: Allen & Unwin.
——. 1958. *Professional Ethics and Civic Morals.* Glencoe, Ill.: Free Press.
——. 1961. *Moral Education.* New York: Free Press of Glencoe.
——. 1964. *The Division of Labor in Society.* New York: Free Press.
Ekeh, Peter. 1974. *Social Exchange Theory: The Two Traditions.* Cambridge, Mass.: Harvard University Press.
Engels, Frederick. 1972. *The Origin of the Family, Private Property and the State.* In Karl Marx and Frederick Engels, *Selected Works.* New York: International Publishers.
——. 1972. *Ludwig Feuerbach and the End of Classical German Philosophy.* In Karl Marx and Frederick Engels, *Selected Works.* New York: International Publishers.
——. 1973. *The Peasant War in Germany.* New York: International Publishers.
——. 1976. *Anti-Duhring.* New York: International Publishers.
Esping-Andersen, Gosta, Roger Friedland, and Erik Olin Wright. 1976. "Modes of Class Struggle and the Capitalist State." *Kapitalistate*, nos. 4–5 (Summer).
Filmer, Paul, et al. 1972. *New Directions in Sociological Theory.* London: Collier, Macmillan.
Frazier, E. Franklin. 1939. *The Negro Family in the United States.* Chicago: University of Chicago Press.
——. 1949. *The Negro in the United States.* New York: Macmillan.
——. 1957. *Race and Culture Contacts in the Modern World.* New York: Knopf.

——. 1957. *Black Bourgeoisie.* Glencoe, Ill.: The Free Press.
Freud, Sigmund. 1949. *An Outline of Psychoanalysis.* New York: Norton.
——. 1950. *The Question of Lay Analysis.* Garden City, N.Y.: Doubleday Anchor.
——. 1961. *The Future of an Illusion.* Garden City, N.Y.: Doubleday Anchor.
——. 1962. *Civilization and Its Discontents.* New York: Norton.
Fromm, Erich. 1962. *Beyond the Chains of Illusion.* New York: Simon and Schuster.
——. 1970. *The Crisis of Psychoanalysis.* New York: Holt Rinehart, Winston.
Garfinkel, Harold. 1967. *Studies in Ethnomethodology.* Englewood Cliffs, N.J.: Prentice-Hall.
Giddens, Anthony. 1971. *Capitalism and Modern Social Theory.* New York: Cambridge University Press.
Goffman, Erving. 1959. *The Presentation of Self in Everyday Life.* Garden City, N.Y.: Doubleday.
——. 1961. *Asylums.* Garden City, N.Y.: Doubleday.
——. 1961. *Encounters.* Indianapolis: Bobbs-Merrill.
——. 1963. *Behavior in Public Places.* New York: Free Press.
——. 1963. *Stigma.* Englewood Cliffs, N.J.: Prentice-Hall.
——. 1967. *Interaction Ritual.* Garden City, N.Y.: Doubleday.
——. 1969. *Strategic Interaction.* New York: Ballantine.
——. 1974. *Frame Analysis.* Cambridge: Harvard University Press.
Gold, David, Clarence Y.H. Lo, and Erik Olin Wright. 1975. "Some Recent Developments in Marxist Theories of the Capitalist State." Pts. 1 and 2. *Monthly Review* 27, nos. 5 and 6 (October and November).
Gouldner, Alvin W. 1970. *The Coming Crisis of Western Sociology.* New York: Avon Books.
Gramsci, Antonio. 1971. *Prison Notebooks.* New York: International Publishers.
——. 1978. *Selections from Political Writings 1921–26.* London: Lawrence & Wishart.
Habermas, Jurgen. 1975. *Legitimation Crisis.* Boston: Beacon Press.
Harvey, David. 1982. *The Limits to Capital.* Cambridge, Mass.: Basil Blackwell.
——. 1990. *The Condition of Postmodernity.* Cambridge, Mass.: Basil Blackwell.
Hegel, G.W.F. 1956. *The Philosophy of History.* New York: Dover.
——. 1969. *Science of Logic.* London: Allen and Unwin.
Holloway, John, and Sol Picciotto. 1977. "Capital, Crisis and the State." *Capital and Class*, no. 2.
——. 1979. "Introduction: Towards a Marxist Theory of the State." In *State and Capital*, ed. John Holloway and Sol Picciotto. London: Edward Arnold.
Homans, George C. 1958. "Social Behavior as Exchange," *American Journal of Sociology* 63.
——. 1961. *Social Behavior: Its Elementary Forms.* New York: Harcourt, Brace and World.
Holt, Alix, ed. 1978. *Selected Writings of Alexandra Kollontai.* Westport, Conn.: Lawrence Hill.
Hopkins, Terence K., and Immanuel Wallerstein. 1982. *World-Systems Analysis.* Beverly Hills, Calif.: Sage Publications.
Horne, Gerald. 1986. *Black & Red: W.E.B. Du Bois and the Afro-American Response to the Cold War, 1944–1963.* Albany, N.Y.: SUNY Press.
Horowitz, Irving Louis, ed. 1963. *Power, Politics and People.* New York: Oxford University Press.
Hume, David. 1949. *A Treatise of Human Nature.* Oxford: Claredon Press.
Jameson, Frederic. 1984. "Postmodernism, or the Cultural Logic of Late Capitalism,' *New Left Review* 146.
Jay, Martin. 1973. *The Dialectical Imagination.* Boston: Little, Brown.
Jessop, Bob. 1982. *The Capitalist State.* New York: New York University Press.
Kant, Immanuel. 1929. *Critique of Pure Reason.* New York: St. Martin's Press.
Kollontai, Alexandra. 1978. "The Social Basis of the Woman Question." In *Selected Writings of Alexandra Kollontai*, Alix Holt. Westport, Conn.: Lawrence Hill.
——. 1978. "Sexual Relations and the Class Struggle." In *Selected Writings of Alexandra Kollontai*, ed. Alix Holt. Westport, Conn.: Lawrence Hill.

Kuhn, Thomas S. 1970. *The Structure of Scientific Revolutions.* 2nd ed. Chicago: University of Chicago Press.
Lenin, V.I. 1947. *Works.* Vol. 31. Moscow: Foreign Languages Publishing House.
——. 1971. *Selected Works.* New York: International Publishers.
——. 1971. *What Is To Be Done?* In V.I. Lenin, Selected Works. New York: International Publishers.
——. 1971. *Imperialism, The Highest Stage of Capitalism.* In V.I. Lenin, *Selected Works.* New York: International Publishers.
——. 1971. *The State and Revolution.* In V.I. Lenin, *Selected Works.* New York: International Publishers.
——. 1974. *The State.* In Karl Marx, Frederick Engels, and V.I. Lenin, *On Historical Materialism.* New York: International Publishers.
——. 1975. *Selected Works in Three Volumes.* Vol. 2. Moscow: Progress Publishers.
Lyotard, Jean-Francois. 1984. *The Postmodern Condition.* Minneapolis: University of Minnesota Press.
McNall, Scott G., ed. 1979. *Theoretical Perspectives in Sociology.* New York: St. Martin's Press.
Manuel, Frank E. 1956. *The New World of Henri Saint-Simon.* Cambridge, Mass.: Harvard University Press.
Marable, Manning. 1986. *W.E.B. Du Bois: Black Radical Democrat.* Boston: Twayne.
Marcuse, Herbert. 1964. *One Dimensional Man.* Boston: Beacon Press.
——. 1968. *Eros and Civilization.* New York: Vintage Books.
Marger, Martin N. 1987. *Elites and Masses: An Introduction to Political Sociology.* 2nd ed. Belmont, Calif.: Wadsworth.
Markham, F.M.H. 1952. *Henri Comte de Saint-Simon.* Oxford, England: Basil Blackwell.
Marx, Karl. 1963. *The Poverty of Philosophy.* New York: International Publishers.
——. 1965. *Pre-Capitalist Economic Formations.* New York: International Publishers.
——. 1967. *Capital.* 3 vols. New York: International Publishers.
——. 1972. "Preface to *A Contribution to the Critique of Political Economy.*" In Karl Marx and Frederick Engels, *Selected Works.* New York: International Publishers.
Marx, K., and F. Engels. 1947. *The German Ideology.* New York: International Publishers.
——. 1972. "Manifesto of the Communist Party." In Karl Marx and Frederick Engels, *Selected Works.* New York: International Publishers.
Mead, George Herbert. 1934. *Mind, Self, and Society.* Chicago: University of Chicago Press.
Meltzer, Bernard N. 1964. *The Social Psychology of George Herbert Mead.* Kalamazoo, Mich.: Western Michigan University Center for Sociological Research.
Meltzer, Bernard N. et al. 1975. *Symbolic Interactionism: Genesis, Varieties and Criticism.* London: Routledge & Kegan Paul.
Merton, Robert K. 1968. *Social Theory and Social Structure.* New York: Free Press.
Michels, Robert. 1968. *Political Parties.* New York: Free Press.
Miliband, Ralph. 1969. *The State in Capitalist Society.* New York: Basic Books.
——. 1970. "The Capitalist State—Reply to Nicos Poulantzas." *New Left Review*, no. 59.
——. 1973. "Poulantzas and the Capitalist State." *New Left Review*, no. 82.
——. 1975. "Political Forms and Historical Materialism." In *Socialist Register, 1975*, ed. R. Miliband and J. Saville. London: Merlin Press.
——. 1977. *Marxism and Politics.* London: Oxford University Press.
——. 1982. *Capitalist Democracy in Britain.* London: Oxford University Press.
Mills, C. Wright. 1951. *White Collar: The American Middle Classes.* New York: Oxford University Press.
——. 1956. *The Power Elite.* New York: Oxford University Press.
——. 1959. *The Sociological Imagination.* New York: Oxford University Press.

Mitchell, Jack N. 1978. *Social Exchange, Dramaturgy, and Ethnomethodology: Toward a Paradigmatic Synthesis.* New York: Elsevier.
Mollenkopf, John. 1975. "Theories of the State and Power Structure Research." *Insurgent Sociologist* 5, no. 3.
Mosca, Gaetano. 1939. *The Ruling Class.* New York: McGraw-Hill.
Oberndorf, C.P. 1953. *A History of Psychoanalysis in America.* New York: Grune.
Palmer, Bryan D. 1990. *Descent into Discourse.* Philadelphia: Temple University Press.
Parenti, Michael. 1970. "Power and Pluralism: The View from the Bottom." *Journal of Politics* 32 (August).
——. 1988. *Democracy for the Few.* 5th ed. New York: St. Martin's Press.
Pareto, Vilfredo. 1935. *The Mind and Society.* 4 vols. New York: Harcourt, Brace.
Parsons, Talcott. 1951. *The Social System.* New York: Free Press.
——. 1960. *Structure and Process in Modern Societies.* New York: Free Press.
——. 1966. *Societies: An Evolutionary Approach.* Englewood Cliffs, N.J.: Prentice Hall.
——. 1967. "On the Concept of Political Power." In T. Parsons, *Sociological Theory and Modern Society.* New York: Free Press.
Picciotto, Sol. 1979. "The Theory of the State, Class Struggle, and the Rule of Law." In *Capitalism and the Rule of Law*, ed. Ben Fine et al. London: Hutchinson.
Platt, Anthony M. 1991. *E. Franklin Frazier Reconsidered.* New Brunswick, N.J.: Rutgers University Press.
Polanyi, Karl. 1957. *The Great Transformation.* Boston: Beacon.
Poulantzas, Nicos. 1969. "The Problem of the Capitalist State." *New Left Review,* no. 58.
——. 1973. *Political Power and Social Classes.* London: Verso.
——. 1974. *Fascism and Dictatorship.* London: New Left Books.
——. 1975. *Classes in Contemporary Capitalism.* London: New Left Books.
——. 1976. *The Crisis of the Dictatorships.* London: New Left Books.
——. 1976. "The Capitalist State: A Reply to Miliband and Laclau." *New Left Review*, no. 95.
——. 1978. *State, Power, Socialism.* London: Verso.
——. 1979. "The Political Crisis and the Crisis of the State." In *Critical Sociology: European Perspectives*, ed. J.W. Freiberg. New York: Irvington.
Reich, Wilhelm. 1949. *Character Analysis.* New York: Orgone Institute Press.
——. 1970. *The Mass Psychology of Fascism.* New York: Farrar, Strauss and Giroux.
——. 1972. *Sex Pol; Essays, 1929–1934.* New York: Random House.
Reynolds, Larry T. 1993. *Interactionism: Exposition and Critique.* Third Edition. Dix Hills, N.Y.: General Hall.
Reynolds, Larry T., and Janice M. Reynolds, eds. 1970. *The Sociology of Sociology.* New York: McKay.
Ross, Robert J.S., and Kent C. Trachte. 1990. *Global Capitalism: The New Leviathan.* Albany, N.Y.: SUNY Press.
Rousseau, Jean Jacques. 1950. *The Social Contract.* New York: Dutton.
Rowbotham, Sheila. 1972. *Women, Resistance, and Revolution.* New York: Penguin.
Saint-Simon, Henri de. 1964. *Social Organization, the Science of Man and Other Writings.* New York.
Skocpol, Theda. 1979. *States and Revolutions: A Comparative Analysis of France, Russia and China.* Cambridge, England: Cambridge University Press.
——. 1981. "Political Response to Capitalist Crisis: Neo-Marxist Theories of the State and the Case of the New Deal." *Politics and Society* 10, no. 2.
Smith, Tony. 1990. *The Logic of Marx's Capital.* Albany, N.Y.: SUNY Press.
So, Alvin Y. 1990. *Social Change and Development.* Newbury Park, Calif.: Sage Publications.
Stryker, Sheldon. 1980. *Symbolic Interactionism.* Menlo Park, Calif.: Benjamin Cummings.

Szymanski, Albert. 1976. "The Revolutionary Uses of Freudian Theory." *Social Praxis* 5, nos. 1–2.

——. 1978. *The Capitalist State and the Politics of Class.* Cambridge, Mass.: Winthrop.

——. 1981. *The Logic of Imperialism.* New York: Praeger.

——. 1983. *Class Structure: A Critical Perspective.* New York: Praeger.

Therborn, Goran. 1976. *Science, Class and Society.* London: New Left Books.

——. 1977. "The Rule of Capital and the Rise of Democracy." *New Left Review*, no. 103.

——. 1978. *What Does the Ruling Class Do When It Rules?* London: New Left Books.

——. 1980. *The Ideology of Power and the Power of Ideology.* London: New Left Books.

——. 1986. "Neo-Marxist, Pluralist, Corporatist, Statist Theories and the Welfare State." In *The State in Global Perspective*, ed. A. Kazancigil. Aldershot, England: Gower and UNESCO.

Trimberger, Ellen K. 1978. *Revolution from Above: Military Bureaucrats and Development in Japan, Turkey, and Peru.* New Brunswick, N.J.: Transaction Books.

Tumin, Melvin. 1953. "Some Principles of Stratification: A Critical Analysis." *American Sociological Review* 18, no. 4 (August).

Turner, Jonathan H. 1978. *The Structure of Sociological Theory.* Homewood, Ill.: Dorsey Press.

Vaughan, Ted R. et al. 1993. *A Critique of Contemporary American Sociology.* Dix Hills, N.Y.: General Hall, Inc.

Wallerstein, Immanuel. 1974. *The Modern World System.* New York: Academic Press.

——. 1974. "The Rise and Future Demise of the World Capitalist System." *Comparative Studies in Society and History* 16 (September).

——. 1979. *The Capitalist World-Economy.* Cambridge, England: Cambridge University Press.

Walton, John. 1990. *Sociology and Critical Inquiry.* 2nd ed. Belmont, Calif.: Wadsworth.

Weber, Max. 1948. *The Protestant Ethic and the Spirit of Capitalism.* New York: Scribners.

——. 1964. *The Theory of Social and Economic Organization.* Edited and with an introduction by Talcott Parsons. New York: Free Press.

——. 1967. *From Max Weber. Essays in Sociology.* Trans., ed., and with an intro. by H.H. Gerth and C. Wright Mills. New York: Oxford University Press.

——. 1968. *Economy and Society.* 3 vols. New York: Bedminster Press.

Weinberg, Meyer, ed. 1970. *W.E.B. Du Bois: A Reader.* New York: Harper & Row.

Wells, Harry K. 1963. *The Failure of Psychoanalysis.* New York: International Publishers.

Westby, David L. 1991. *The Growth of Sociological Theory.* Englewood Cliffs, N.J.: Prentice Hall.

Willie, Charles V., ed. 1989. *The Caste and Class Controversy on Race and Poverty*, Second Edition. Dix Hills, N.Y.: General Hall.

Wilson, William Julius. 1980. *The Declining Significance of Race*, Second Edition. Chicago: University of Chicago Press.

——. 1987. *The Truly Disadvantaged: The Inner City, the Underclass, and Public Policy.* Chicago: University of Chicago Press.

Wolff, Kurt H., ed. 1960. *Emile Durkheim, 1858–1917.* Columbus: Ohio State University Press.

Wright, Erik Olin. 1974–75. "To Control or To Smash Bureaucracy: Weber and Lenin on Politics, the State, and Bureaucracy." *Berkeley Journal of Sociology* 19.

——. 1978. *Class, Crisis and the State.* London: New Left Books.

——. 1985. *Classes.* London: Verso.

Zeitlin, Irving M. 1968. *Ideology and the Development of Sociological Theory.* Englewood Cliffs, N.J.: Prentice Hall.

——. 1973. *Rethinking Sociology: A Critique of Contemporary Sociology.* Englewood Cliffs, N.J.: Prentice Hall.

——. 1981. *The Social Condition of Humanity.* New York: Oxford University Press.

——. 1997. *Ideology and the Development of Sociological Theory.* Sixth Edition. Upper Saddle River, N.J.: Prentice Hall.

ABOUT THE AUTHOR

Berch Berberoglu is Foundation Professor and Chair of the Department of Sociology at the University of Nevada, Reno, where he has been teaching for the past twenty years.

Dr. Berberoglu has authored and edited fifteen books and many articles in numerous scholarly journals. His recent books include *The Internationalization of Capital* (1987), *Political Sociology: A Comparative/Historical Approach* (1990), *Critical Perspectives in Sociology* (1991 and 1993), *The Legacy of Empire: Economic Decline and Class Polarization in the United States* (1992), *The Political Economy of Development* (1992), *The Labor Process and Control of Labor: The Changing Nature of Work Relations in the Late 20th Century* (1993), *Class Structure and Social Transformation* (1994), and *The National Question: Nationalism, Ethnic Conflict, and Self-Determination in the 20th Century* (1995).

He is currently doing research and writing on nationalism and ethnic conflict for his forthcoming book *Class, State, and Nation: The Class Nature of Nationalism and Ethnic Conflict* and is preparing a new book-length manuscript *The State and Revolution in the 20th Century*, scheduled for publication in 1998 and 1999, respectively.

Dr. Berberoglu received his Ph.D. from the University of Oregon in 1977 and his B.S. and M.A. from Central Michigan University in 1972 and 1974.

INDEX